CHRISTMAS *with the* FIRST LADIES

THE WHITE HOUSE DECORATING TRADITION FROM
Jacqueline Kennedy TO *Michelle Obama*

By Coleen Christian Burke

FOREWORD BY DEBORAH NORVILLE

INSIGHT EDITIONS

SAN RAFAEL, CA

Library of Congress Cataloging-in-Publication Data available.
ISBN: 978-1-60887-046-2

PHOTO CREDITS: **White House/John. F. Kennedy Presidential Library and Museum:** Robert Knudsen (pages 11, 12, 16, 21); Abbie Rowe (pages 15, 17); Cecil W. Stoughton (pages 14, 19, 20, 22, 23). **Lyndon B. Johnson Library and Museum:** Robert Knudsen (page 27, 31); Cecil W. Stoughton (page 29); Unknown (page 30); Frank Wolfe (page 32, 36–37); Yoichi Okamoto (pages 33, 34); Mike Geissinger (page 35). **Nixon Presidential Library and Museum:** Robert Knudsen (page 41); Jack Kightlinger (pages 42, 44, 46–48, 51); Oliver Atkins (pages 45, 53); K. Schumacher (page 52). **Gerald R. Ford Presidential Library:** Karl Schumacher (pages 57, 59, 61–63, 65–67); Bill Fitz-Patrick (page 60). **Jimmy Carter Library:** Jack Kightlinger (page 71); Karl Schumacher (pages 72, 74–75, 81); Mary Anne Fackelman (page 76); Bill Fitz-Patrick (page 78); Unknown (page 79); Dailey (page 80). **Ronald Reagan Presidential Library:** Bill Fitz-Patrick (pages 85, 89); Mary Anne Fackelman (pages 86, 88, 92–93, 95); Pete Souza (pages 90–91); Jack Kightlinger (page 94). **George Bush Presidential Library and Museum:** Joyce Naltchayan (pages 99, 102–104, 106); Carol Powers (pages 101, 107, 109); David Valdez (page 105); Susan Biddle (page 108). **William J. Clinton Presidential Library:** Sharon Farmer (pages 112, 114, 119, 124); Ralph Alswang (pages 7, 116–118, 122); William Vista (page 120–121); Barbara Kinney (page 125). **George W. Bush Presidential Library:** Shealah Craighead (pages 9, 129, 134, 140); Chris Greenberg (page 130); Tina Hager (pages 132, 133); Susan Sterner (pages 37, 135, 136); Paul Morse (page 139); Eric Draper (page 141). **The White House:** Pete Souza (pages 145, 148); Chuck Kennedy (pages 147, 149, 157); Samantha Appleton (page 150); Lawrence Jackson (pages 151–153, 155,156). **Original Craft/Recipe Photos:** Anne Marie Caruso and Michael Peter Karas. Food Stylist: Maureen Petrosky.

Excerpt on pages 73, 76, 79 reprinted with permission from First Lady Rosalynn Carter from *First Lady From Plains*, University of Arkansas Press. Copyright 1984 by Rosalynn Carter.
Excerpt on pages 58, 61, 63 reprinted with permission from First Lady Betty Ford from *The Times of My Life*. Copyright 1978 by Betty Ford.
Excerpt on pages 28, 31, 36 reprinted with permission from LBJ Library & Museum from *A White House Diary* by Lady Bird Johnson. Copyright 1970.

REPLANTED PAPER

Insight Editions, in association with Roots of Peace, will plant two trees for each tree used in the manufacturing of this book. Roots of Peace is an internationally renowned humanitarian organization dedicated to eradicating land mines worldwide and converting war-torn lands into productive farms and wildlife habitats. Together, we will plant two million fruit and nut trees in Afghanistan and provide farmers there with the skills and support necessary for sustainable land use.

Manufactured in China by Insight Editions
www.insighteditions.com

10 9 8 7 6 5 4 3 2

INSIGHT EDITIONS
P.O. Box 3088, San Rafael, CA 94912
www.insighteditions.com

Dedication

TO JERRY, MAEVE, J., AND BRENNA—FOR ALL THE CHRISTMAS MAGIC;

TO MY GRANDPARENTS,
MARGE AND ED TODD—FOR ALL THE CHRISTMAS LOVE;

TO MY DAD,
DAVID A. CHRISTIAN—FOR GIVING ME A PASSION FOR POLITICS;

AND TO MY MOM,
PEGGY—THANK YOU FOR SHOWING ME THE WONDER OF CHRISTMAS DECORATING.
I COULDN'T HAVE WRITTEN THIS BOOK WITHOUT YOU.

ACKNOWLEDGMENTS

I'd like to thank my amazing husband, Jerry Burke, for sharing my love of history and for his extraordinary skill as a copy editor. And to my children, Maeve, J., and Brenna, for inspiring me to write this book—you three are more beautiful than the fanciest Christmas decoration.

To my parents, Peggy and David Christian, thank you for teaching me to believe in myself. I certainly set my sights high when I decided to Christmas decorate as elegantly as Mom. (Still trying, by the way.)

To First Lady Laura and President Bush, for inviting me to decorate the White House for Christmas. It will always remain one of the great honors of my life. To former White House Chief Floral Designer Nancy Clarke, for welcoming me to the decorating team. And to former White House press secretary Ari Fleisher, for being my biggest supporter in my dream to decorate 1600 Pennsylvania Avenue.

To my sister Maureen Petrosky, for your impeccable taste and fabulous culinary skills. To my sister K. C., for your invaluable technical guidance and willingness to drop everything whenever I called for help. And to my brother Dave, for everything that comes next.

This book wouldn't have happened without power-couple George and Margaret Uribe and their amazing knack for networking, which led me to my superstar literary agent Nena Madonia. Many thanks to Nena and her boss Jan Miller of DMA for believing in this project and bringing it to the attention of Jake Gerli of Insight Editions. Thank you, Jake, for thinking that a picture of Mr. T at the White House is as hilarious as I do.

Many thanks to the incredibly talented team that Insight Editions publisher, Raoul Goff, put together for this project: Jan Hughes, Jason Babler, Stephanie Orma, Deborah Kops, Anne Marie Caruso, and Michael Peter Karas. Special thanks to my wonderful managing editor, Kevin Toyama, and fabulous editor Micaela Heekin, who both always knew the exact right thing to say and do.

To Jen and Rich Lange and Megan Lander, for always helping when I called. To Joanne LaMarca, for giving me the advice that got this book published. To Kimberley Clearwater, for letting me hijack her life for photo shoots. To my Villanova professors, Dr. Jack Doody and Dr. Colleen Sheehan, for teaching me the power of thoughts and words. To Myrtle Elmore, for imparting cranberry tree knowledge. To Jodie Steck, Pamla Eisenberg, Nancy Mirshah, Maryrose Grossman, Michael Pinckney, Tim Holtz, and Amy Owens for limitless help. To my Grandmother Margaret Todd, my Godmother Dorothea Christian, and my mother-in-law, Frances Burke, for being my cheerleaders.

To Deborah Norville, for sharing advice and giving of her time.

And *finally*, to my media buddies Steven Lerner, Jeremy Spiegel, Stacey Reiss, Lucy Segal, Cordelia Bowe, Lynn Doyle, Diane Dimond, and Michael Schoen for encouraging me to try new things. *Thank you all.*

Table of
CONTENTS

Foreword by
DEBORAH NORVILLE

Coleen Christian Burke and I have been friends since we worked together on the television show *Inside Edition*. She left television to follow her passion for decorating, so I was thrilled when she was invited to be a part of the White House decorating team. Awed by the history of the place that she was helping to transform, and ever the reporter, Coleen began tracking down White House Christmas traditions.

Christmas is a magical time no matter where you spend it. But at the White House, the spirit of the season knows no bounds. The gorgeous trees and beautiful ornaments reflect the extraordinary creativity and design know-how of many craftspeople and decorators. Nativity crèches, natural flowers, antique toys, fresh-baked treats—just about everything has served as a holiday motif at the White House.

Starting with the Kennedy era, Coleen recounts White House Christmases of the past half century. As one White House social secretary put it, the holidays at the White House are a battle that is months in the planning. The President's wife may have lots of soldiers, but she's still the general

directing the troops. With all that help, one would think the First Ladies breezed through Christmas, but that's rarely the case. Jacqueline Kennedy armed herself with detailed Christmas lists. Hillary Clinton was informed in June of her first year in the White House that she was already *behind* on her Christmas planning! One thing becomes readily apparent when you're reading this book: When it comes to celebrating Christmas, the occupants of the White House really aren't that different from the rest of us.

Coleen and I share not only a love of journalism but also of handicrafts. Some of my most cherished Christmas remembrances are connected with homemade gifts and decorations that I have created or received. In the following chapters you will find inspired ways to create the Christmas looks of the First Ladies through their stories, crafts, and recipes. Perhaps Mrs. Johnson, who commissioned ornaments featuring flowers from all fifty states, will inspire you to create a holiday arrangement paying tribute to the lands of your forebears. Maybe the personalized gingerbread houses of the

Reagan years will encourage you to go beyond the simple tiny cottage you usually create.

And what is Christmas without a tree? The Obamas had twenty-seven trees their first Christmas at 1600 Pennsylvania Avenue!

At the White House, the spirit of the season knows no bounds. The gorgeous trees and beautiful ornaments reflect the extraordinary creativity and design know-how of many craftspeople and decorators.

No doubt that's more than at your house, but perhaps you do trim more than one tree during the holidays. At my house the fancy tree in the living room is color-coordinated to match the decor of the room, while the "real" tree in the family room is hung with a hodgepodge of ornaments made in kindergarten or passed down from beloved family members. Jacqueline Kennedy did the same, presiding over the design of a lavish tree in the Blue Room of the White House, while the family lovingly decorated their own tree themselves.

Each chapter ends with a how-to craft or special recipe straight from the First Lady's personal file. Whether it's Lady Bird Johnson's cranberry salad, Nancy Reagan's famed monkey bread, or Michelle Obama's gingerbread ornaments, you'll find plenty here to bring a bit of the White House to *your* house. So as you settle down to read, make yourself a cup of tea, let your imagination run wild, and let me be the first to wish you "Merry Christmas!"

INTRODUCTION

In December 2008, at the invitation of First Lady Laura Bush, I had the privilege of walking through an employee entrance to begin a day of Christmas decorating at the most prestigious home in America—the White House. Armed with wire cutters and floral wire, I happily took on any task the White House Chief Floral Designer Nancy Clarke assigned to me—including climbing rickety twenty-foot scaffolding to decorate the green roping that adorned the huge doorways in the East Room.

As I worked with bows, bunting, and ornaments, I was ever aware of the historical importance of the rooms in which I stood. I imagined the Presidents, the parties, and as a Christmas decorator, the holiday decor that had unfolded in those places. When the halls were finally decked after two exhausting days, Mrs. Bush thanked the volunteer decorators by inviting us to the first Christmas party of the season. As I entered the White House, this time through the official visitor's entrance, I was able to experience the holiday decorations as thousands of others would experience them. I heard the sounds of the President's band playing, and a Marine greeted me with the words, "Merry Christmas and welcome to the White House." I was very proud to have played a part in preparing the White House for Christmas. The next day I was even prouder to watch the *Today* show with my three young children, as the holiday decor I had worked on was unveiled to the nation.

During my time at 1600 Pennsylvania Avenue, Christmas decorating traditions at the White House were a popular topic of discussion among us decorators. As we adorned the trees, bits and pieces of information emerged. I learned that Jackie Kennedy, the wife of John F. Kennedy, the first Catholic President, had a major impact on Christmas decor. She believed that for Christmas at the White House, personal and thoughtful consideration must be given to decorating decisions on a religious and secular level. Mrs. Kennedy declared that holiday decorations must be unified, and she achieved her goal by selecting an annual Christmas theme. The First Ladies who followed Mrs. Kennedy have continued this tradition. They have personally selected Christmas themes, creating a rich heritage of holiday celebration and decoration stretching over fifty years.

With my curiosity piqued, I embarked on an intriguing journey to learn more about White House Christmas decorating, starting with Mrs. Kennedy and continuing on through the years to our current First Lady, Michelle Obama. Utilizing presidential libraries, I poked my head into files and boxes and photos from our past. Suddenly, my house was a very exciting place to be, as the caller

As I worked with bows, bunting, and ornaments, I was ever aware of the historical importance of the rooms in which I stood.

ID announced names like John F. Kennedy, Richard Nixon, and Ronald Reagan, and packages from Lady Bird Johnson, Mrs. Ford, and Mrs. Carter appeared on my porch. The libraries were always helpful. Each box I received

from them was like a treasure chest, as I never knew what would be inside. Much of the information and memorabilia from Christmases past had not been officially catalogued, and so much of what I received and am now sharing with you hadn't been viewed outside of the libraries' archives.

What I was not expecting to find during my search was evidence of the intimate, private Christmas celebrations of our First Families. Although these moments were purposely recorded for history, for the most part the records have sat undisturbed in archives. These private celebrations, when compared with the public Christmas events, give us real insight into the White House—the families, the formalities, and the fabulous decor.

Mrs. Kennedy's original concept of a Christmas theme has certainly evolved over the last five decades. The early themes were understated, repeated in subsequent Christmas seasons, and sometimes even went unnamed until after the fact. Today the themes are spelled out, and the decorating vision of the First Lady is executed with professional precision and aplomb.

This book is my holiday gift to you. It will give you a special glimpse inside the White House at Christmas; but more than that, it will also show you how to copy the holiday secrets and decorating tips of our First Ladies in your home this Christmas.

1

First Lady of Christmas

JACQUELINE KENNEDY

1961–1963

Jacqueline Kennedy

"Hello, Mrs. Santa Claus—I mean, Mrs. Kennedy."

—FIVE-YEAR-OLD PATIENT, DISTRICT OF COLUMBIA CHILDREN'S HOSPITAL,
QUOTED IN THE *WASHINGTON POST*

With her fashionable red Christmas suits and accompanying mink beret, it seems funny that the glamorous First Lady could be confused with Mrs. Claus, even by a little boy. But that's what happened when Jacqueline, or "Jackie," as she was affectionately called, Kennedy visited the District of Columbia's Children's Hospital to wish sick children a Merry Christmas. Although he was confused, the little boy was actually quite insightful. Mrs. Kennedy embodied both the height of cultural sophistication and understated simplicity. She was an icon of style, but she had a bit of cozy Mrs. Claus in her as well.

In 1961 the very first White House Christmas theme was the "Nutcracker." The "Nutcracker" theme reflected Jackie Kennedy's love of ballet, classical music, and culture. Central to the story of the *Nutcracker* ballet is a majestic Victorian Christmas tree. Jackie had her version of the *Nutcracker* tree displayed in the Blue Room, its great height just clearing the ceiling when the tree was topped with a star. Blue ribbon crisscrossed the tree branches, which were lit with small artificial candles in place of the real candles that were used in the 1800s. Large snowflakes hung next to miniature candy canes, baskets, angels, and birds and other animals.

Mrs. Kennedy worked hard putting together plans for two distinct Christmas experiences. The first was the public White House experience, which she thought should have a polished and professional look. The second was the private Kennedy Christmas, which would be celebrated each year in Palm Beach, Florida. For many years, Jack and Jackie spent Christmas in the home of JFK's parents, Joe and Rose Kennedy. Later, when they needed more room, they stayed at the private oceanfront home of their family friend Colonel C. Michael Paul. These Kennedy Christmases were very different in tone from Christmas at the White House. They were informal, spontaneous, and even a little haphazard.

As the Kennedys prepared for their first White House Christmas season, Mrs. Kennedy took great care with gift selection. As early as September 1961, a letter to the U.S. embassy in Paris indicates beautiful Chanel chiffon scarves were found and purchased for Mrs. Kennedy to give as presents. Mrs. Kennedy

PRECEDING SPREAD :: President and Mrs. Kennedy stop in front of the official Christmas tree during a White House Christmas reception, 1962.
LEFT :: President and Mrs. Kennedy unveil the very first White House Christmas Theme, the "Nutcracker," 1961.

also explored the idea of having leather-bound scrapbooks made, as well as a bound collection of inaugural speeches published. She had prototypes of each gift designed, but ultimately decided against both projects because of the cost. Still, she very much liked the idea of the book of inaugural speeches, and saved that idea for a future Christmas.

Because Mrs. Kennedy planned to leave with the children in mid-December for Palm Beach, the White House events for December 1961 were limited. President and Mrs. Kennedy attended a modest party for the White House residence staff and their families on December 13. Staffers received several presents from the First Couple. The first was a photo of Caroline's pet ducks playing in the pond on the South Lawn, with the White House in the background. The second was a print of the

official Christmas card displayed in a red leather folder, complete with the Presidential Seal on the front. In a sign of simpler times, donated candy canes were displayed, fifty at a time, on a lone table in the vast East Room. These were parting gifts to the staff's children.

Mrs. Kennedy left for Palm Beach on December 14, opting not to attend a special event she herself had created—the Diplomatic Chil-

Donated candy canes, parting gifts for the staff's children were displayed on a lone table in the vast East Room.

dren's Party, which would become a Christmas custom for years to come. Although she was in Florida, Mrs. Kennedy had signed off on the plans for the party. As with the Residence Staff Party, minimal decoration went

ABOVE :: The Kennedy's 1962 Christmas card shows Caroline's horse Macaroni pulling Mrs. Kennedy, Caroline, and John-John in a sled across the White House south lawn.

RIGHT :: Young Caroline Kennedy spies the Blue Room tree in 1961.

into the festivities: A balloon was tied to each child's chair and a simple centerpiece of a stuffed Santa was placed in the center of each round table.

Not long after the Kennedys arrived in Palm Beach, the jovial holiday mood turned somber. The President's father, Ambassador Joe Kennedy, suffered a stroke on December 19. On Christmas Day, Jack attended mass at the hospital while Jackie stayed with

For Christmas 1962, Mrs. Kennedy chose the theme of the "Children's Tree."

the children. Caroline played with her new toys, which included a plastic set of horses, complete with a barn. At just one year old, the press noted, John Jr. was too young to open presents. The family took turns visiting

Joe, whose condition improved, although he never fully regained his speech.

The next year was a busy one for Mrs. Kennedy. She had begun redecorating the White House, a major undertaking. In a televised tour in February, the First Lady showcased the transformation of some of the state rooms.

For Christmas 1962, Mrs. Kennedy chose the theme of the "Children's Tree." She wanted to capture the wonder of Christmas for the nation's youngest citizens. But it was also important to Mrs. Kennedy to include the religious meaning of the holiday. Along with the theme of the "Children's Tree," Jackie wanted a crèche, or Nativity scene, complete with biblical statues.

Mrs. Kennedy expressed her wish for an awe-inspiring crèche to her social secretary, Letitia Baldrige. Letitia had previously worked at Tiffany and remembered an impressive crèche that was once displayed in the store. She reached out to the owner:

> ᴄ~ I therefore dare to ask if we could borrow a group of your Neapolitan crèche figures for the Christmas season at the White House. They would be placed in a prominent position, but safe from reaching hands. Since I know it is difficult to turn down the President or the First Lady, I would like to say that neither of them in all honesty know I am making this request of you. ~ᴐ

Of course the crèche was lent! It was displayed in the East Room, flanked by curtains and surrounded by white azaleas. With the issue of the crèche resolved, the 1962 "Children's Tree" was placed in the Grand Foyer because of the ongoing renovation of the Blue Room. The star remained atop the tree, but gone was the blue ribbon of the previous year. A small tree skirt of green moss circled the base. Many of the miniature ornaments were back, and new ones were added: tiny twig stars, little wrapped Christmas boxes, reindeer, candy canes, and stuffed animals. Humpty Dumpty found his way to the tree, as did a tiny PT boat, hung to honor the President's heroism in World War II.

The Residence Staff Party was a festive affair in 1962. The Army Chorus, Navy Sea Chanters, and Air Force Singing Sergeants caroled through the Cross Hall. Although they were more than half an hour late, the First Couple seemed to enjoy the party, and

LEFT :: In 1962, the crèche was displayed in the East Room and surrounded by azaleas.

PAGE 19 :: The President and Mrs. Kennedy watch Caroline, John-John, and a friend reenact the nativity scene in Palm Beach in 1962.

gave each member of the staff a commemorative 15-by-17-inch print of a watercolor of the Red Room by the artist Edward Lehman. Each was personally signed by both the President and First Lady. (Reporters noted that the President's autograph was worth fifty dollars.) A week

Many of the miniature ornaments were back, and new ones were added: tiny twig stars, little wrapped Christmas boxes, reindeer, candy canes, and stuffed animals.

later, each employee also received a picture of Caroline's horse, Macaroni, pulling Mrs. Kennedy and the children across the White House's South Lawn in a sleigh. The picture was used for the Kennedy's official 1962 Christmas card, and was meant to be given out at the staff party, but was forgotten amid all the revelry.

```
                    Dec. 12, 1962
          Christmas Gifts List

          Mrs. Kennedy,

  Following is a list of presents that will be kept
          close to you—by plane to Palm Beach:

  2 Guidebooks—one initialed one from the President
  to Ambassador Kennedy and one to the Ambassador and
  Mrs. Kennedy signed by you and the President

      Guidebook for Prince and Princess Radziwell
          Engraving for Anthony Radziwell
      "          "    Christina Radziwell
  Set of [Jacqueline] Duheme sketches for Anthony
                    and Christina
      Engraving, check and coat for Provy
        Engraving, check for Miss Shaw
      Engraving and check for George Thomas

              Boat for John Jr.
            Parrot for Caroline
            Drums for each child
      Mary Poppins books for Caroline (5)
      Plasti-Figura (game) for Caroline
          Chilean saddle for Caroline

            Teddy Bear for John Jr.
  1 box of felt figurines dolls and animals for Tony and
                      Tina
        1 doll rocking chair for Caroline
  2 very small handmade doll chairs for Caroline
          Stuffed animals for John Jr.
```

As was the custom, Mrs. Kennedy and the children left for Palm Beach the day after the Residence Staff Party. That year she took a "Christmas Gifts List" with her.

Although it is unknown who wrote the list for Mrs. Kennedy, it's comforting to know that even the First Lady needed a cheat sheet at Christmas to keep everything straight. The guidebooks mentioned in the list were leather-bound copies of "The White House: A Historic Guide," which Mrs. Kennedy had commissioned from the White House Historical Association. The engravings were of President Kennedy's favorite painting, William H. Bartlett's *The President's House*. All the gifts were certain to be treasured by the Kennedy family and the Radziwell family (Jackie's sister's family), and appreciated by Provy, Miss Shaw, and George Thomas, the Kennedys' trusted longtime employees.

The Palm Beach Christmas of 1962 appeared to be a magical one, judging from the intimate photos captured by the President's photographer. President Kennedy hung white stockings trimmed with pompoms, which were made for the Kennedy family when John was born. Each stocking was embroidered with a different, specially chosen scene. Caroline, age five, and John, age two, played with their cousins Tony and Tina. All four children acted out the Pageant of Peace, or birth of Christ, in costume for their parents. Jackie, in a perfect red leisure suit with matching sandals and manicured toes, smoked a cigarette as she watched the

performance. In the corner, a hastily decorated tree heralded the holiday. Lopsided red candles lined the mantel.

The family woke the next morning to a Christmas Day filled with activities. Jackie gave the President an antique scrimshaw, or whalebone carved by a whaler. The family spent the afternoon sailing on the presidential yacht, *The Honey Fitz.* Mrs. Kennedy took advantage of the beautiful Christmas weather and even went waterskiing! Later, an eggnog party preceded the holiday dinner, which usually included a Massachusetts-raised turkey, baked grapefruit, cranberry sauce, sweet potatoes, and chocolate and vanilla ice cream.

Plans for Christmas 1963 were well underway by the fall of that year, including Mrs. Kennedy's gift to the Secret Service. The social secretary Nancy Tuckerman noted, "She would like to give the men polo shirts, and prefers the type with short sleeves and an alligator design. The colors she has chosen are black, navy, light blue, white and gray. There are 70 Secret Service Men, and 20 shirts should be large and 50 extra large."

The artist Edward Lehman was again called upon to make a watercolor that was to be given to the residence staff. This time it would be of the newly renovated Green Room, which was refurbished with American antique furniture and priceless paintings. And Mrs. Kennedy finally decided to commission that bound edition of the collected presidential inaugural addresses.

FAR LEFT :: President Kennedy hangs Christmas stockings with John Jr. and a friend in Palm Beach in 1962.

LEFT :: This shows the front of the Christmas card that Mrs. Kennedy had printed in the fall of 1963. Few have seen the card because all but a few were destroyed after the President's assassination.

For Mrs. Kennedy's early foray into book publishing, she chose block letters for the cover and marbleized endpapers inside.

But it was the First Lady's public Christmas efforts that set the country abuzz. Mrs. Kennedy was an artist in her own right, and in

It was Mrs. Kennedy's public Christmas efforts that set the country abuzz, when she teamed up with Hallmark to design her own cards.

1963 she teamed up with Hallmark to design her own Christmas cards. The cards would be sold wherever Hallmark cards were available, and the proceeds would go toward the proposed thirty-million-dollar cultural center in Washington, DC. The First Lady designed two different styles: The first was called "The Journey of the Magi" and featured the three wise men on camels. The second was an angel with a trumpet, with the message "Glad Tidings" printed inside. Both cards were signed "JBK" in the lower right corner. By mid-November, the First Lady's cards were flying off the shelves, and storekeepers were promising their customers that they would surely get more.

In addition to working on the Hallmark cards, Mrs. Kennedy selected the official White House Christmas cards from Mrs. Kennedy and the President. They featured a beautiful photo of the Neapolitan crèche, still on loan to the White House. The inscription beneath the Presidential Seal read, "With our wishes for a Blessed Christmas and a Happy New Year." By November 1963, both the President and Jackie had already signed about thirty of them.

The Kennedys' plans for Christmas at the White House came to an abrupt and tragic halt with the crack of an assassin's rifle on November 22, 1963. With the President's sudden death, there would be no Christmas theme or Residence Staff Party. Still, Jackie, now a widow, would have Christmas. She had her children to consider.

In the aftermath of the President's assassination, all but a few of the crèche Christmas cards were destroyed. Jackie's Christmas cards for Hallmark sold out, never to be restocked, with the proceeds now going to the newly named Kennedy Center. Jackie gave the Edward Lehman print of the Green Room to the residence staff. The bound editions of the inaugural speeches went to their

ABOVE :: Candid Christmas moments with Mrs. Kennedy and her children in Palm Beach in 1962.

intended recipients. One was for Boston's Richard Cardinal Cushing. The *Boston Globe* reported that Jackie inscribed it:

> Jack was going to give you this for Christmas. Please accept it now from me. With my devotion always— for all you were to our "dear Jack" and to me.

Jackie took the children to Palm Beach. She attempted to go Christmas shopping with her brother-in-law Bobby but the people crowding around her forced them to go home. A sailing trip on *The Honey Fitz* was canceled because of bad weather.

On Christmas morning at the Kennedy family home, Jackie visited with Joe and Rose and Jack's sister Eunice Shriver and her husband, Sargent. Later, when she wanted to

return to the Paul estate, where she was staying, a second car was needed to carry all the presents for Caroline and John. More than 150 people waited that Christmas Day to wave at the widow, and when she saw them she waved back, making her way with the gifts for her now fatherless children. One of the toys was a bright red fire truck for Caroline from Luci Baines, the new President's daughter.

As First Lady, Mrs. Kennedy had two seasons of Christmas wonder and one of unbearable loss. She proudly witnessed President Kennedy's powerful legacy—including his support for civil rights legislation and the early successes of the space program—take root. For her part, the First Lady of Camelot left an equally lasting mark on the White House. Her style and impeccable taste were legendary, and the tradition she began with her Christmas themes continues today.

WHAT'S *She* WEARING?

In 1960 it wasn't just the details of Mrs. Kennedy's holiday wardrobe that people were clamoring to learn about. The American public also wanted to know what Caroline and John Jr. would be wearing for Christmas. John was born on November 25, and while the First Lady was recovering, Caroline was whisked away to the Estelle Parker Shop in Boston for a shopping trip with her governess. The First Daughter picked out seventy items (over which Jackie had final say), including her Christmas dress, which was white organdy with rosebuds and ribbons. A tiny shirt and shorts outfit with a Christmas tree stitched on the shirt pocket was purchased for Johnny. (Interestingly, the name John-John hadn't stuck yet, and newspapers were calling the baby Johnny!)

Jacqueline Kennedy's
ENCHANTED CHRISTMAS-PRESENT TREE

In my version of Mrs. Kennedy's Christmas-Present Tree (pictured left), I re-created the endearing "tiny present" ornaments she hung on her tree. Mrs. Kennedy's ornaments were much smaller than those used by subsequent First Ladies and appear almost miniature, given the scale of the White House. This ornament is a square cardboard box that's available at most craft stores and is wrapped with festive paper.

Supplies

Scissors

Wrapping paper, 1 or 2 papers (see Tips)

Small boxes

Cellophane tape

Trinkets (optional)

Narrow ribbon, ½ inch wide or less (see Tips)

Gold or silver cord

Tips :: It is best to limit yourself to one or two different papers. You may want to choose a patterned paper and a solid colored paper to make the greatest impact. The ribbon is the unifying element, and the same ribbon should be used on all of the presents.

STEP *One* Using the scissors, cut the paper and wrap your boxes; secure with the tape. For a modern twist, put a small trinket or treat inside a few of the boxes before you wrap them. Make sure to mark the boxes containing trinkets so they are easily identified on the tree.

STEP *Two* Embellish the presents by tying them with the ribbon once horizontally and once vertically, as is the custom. Be sure to finish them with a ribbon bow.

STEP *Three* Slide the gold or silver cord under the ribbon on the side of the box, and hang the present on the tree. Repeat with the remaining presents.

STEP *Four* Have holiday guests pick a present from the tree to see if they win a trinket!

2

From Tragedy to a White House Wedding

LADY BIRD JOHNSON

1963–1969

FROM TRAGEDY TO A WHITE HOUSE WEDDING
Lady Bird Johnson

"Gone is the black mourning crepe that swathed the great chandeliers in the State Rooms and draped the high doorways. The flags, at half-mast this long month, now rise and with them my spirits. The sense of pall that held the house in hushed quiet has lifted, and we can begin to turn our eyes to Christmas!"

—LADY BIRD JOHNSON • 12.23.63 • FROM *A WHITE HOUSE DIARY*

On December 23, 1963, Lady Bird Johnson donned her Christmas red in a bold move that welcomed Christmas to the White House and ended the official period of mourning for President John F. Kennedy. The black mourning crepe came down, and Mrs. Johnson herself put away her mourning dresses. If there was ever a time Christmas at the White House was necessary, it was 1963.

By bringing out her holiday red, the new First Lady chose her course—she would help the nation face its future, and she would start with Christmas. Mrs. Johnson was careful to honor the holiday in a way that was respectful of the slain President. She requested only live evergreens to decorate the White House, and no Christmas theme was chosen. As the holiday neared, the Johnsons headed to their Texas ranch for Christmas Day 1963, a pattern they would repeat for the next three years.

Following the muted Christmas of 1963, Mrs. Johnson chose the theme of "Early Americana" for both 1964 and 1965. The decorations both years featured greens and fruit and were very similar. In 1965 the massive doorways of the state rooms were hung with garland made of huckleberries, apples, lemons, plums, and lollipops. Visitors had to be careful not to be caught under the mistletoe, sent from the Johnsons' home state of Texas and hung in abundance throughout the White House.

The official Blue Room tree in 1965 was decorated with nuts, popcorn, and cranberry chains; straw stars; bunches of geraniums; toy soldiers; and gingerbread ornaments. Altogether there were three thousand ornaments hanging when the tree was finally finished. Mrs. Johnson loved the Blue Room tree, writing in her published diary, "There were garlands of popcorn and miracles of lights. It was a beautiful work of art."

The gingerbread ornaments—in the shape of Santas, camels, snowmen, teddy bears, dolls, and hearts—delighted all who

PRECEDING PAGE :: Lady Bird and LBJ pose in front of the Blue Room tree in 1966. RIGHT :: Mrs. Kennedy and Mrs. Johnson look on as President Johnson gives one of his first speeches in the East Room in December of 1963. Note the black mourning bunting that was hung as a tribute to President Kennedy.

came to see the tree. These ornaments had a secret, which Mrs. Johnson loved to tell visitors—the gingerbread ornaments hanging on the lower branches were real, while the ones on the higher branches were ceramic look-alikes. Lady Bird's social secretary, Bess Abel, noted in a letter, "After one children's party I noticed a missing leg from a gingerbread man hanging on a lower branch. On closer inspection I could see tiny teeth marks left by a nibbler."

The gingerbread ornaments—in the shape of Santas, camels, snowmen, teddy bears, dolls, and hearts—delighted all who came to see the tree.

By 1966, America was erupting with race riots and anti–Vietnam War demonstrations. But the social unrest outside the White House had no impact on Christmas plans. Whether Mrs. Johnson sought comfort in the past, or merely loved the tradition of Americana, she built on that theme again that year, and would continue to do so in 1967 and 1968. The fundamental decorations stayed the same, with new items added each Christmas. In 1966, for example, the White House received a beautiful wreath from the great-great-great-granddaughter of Chief Sitting Bull. Scenes from the Twelve Days of Christmas decorated the large North Portico mirror.

Mrs. Johnson's impassioned desire to conserve nature and beautify America with flowers had the most impact on Christmas decorations in 1966. Hundreds of bright yellow, orange, red, and blue flowers were cut from felt and hung on the Blue Room tree. The decor included a large, impressive State Flower Wreath, made with flowers from all fifty states.

Over the years a series of children's parties had become customary. There were parties for the children of members of Congress, the children of the residence staff, and underprivileged children. And finally, there was the Diplomatic Children's Party. Under Mrs. Johnson, the entertainment at these parties included Bavarian folk dancers, Polish wedding dancers, and the Army's Old Guard Fife and Drum Corps, complete with wigs and period costumes.

The White House press secretary, Sandy Fox, played Santa in 1966, and First Daughters Luci and Lynda helped hand out presents. Low tables and child-size chairs were set up in the State Dining Room, and cookies and ice

cream were served. Despite the dignified surroundings, these events were uproarious. "Thomas Jefferson and James Madison rocked in their frames, the Christmas tree in the Blue Room teetered, Santa Claus wiped his brow and staggered back. The children's invasion of the White House was over for another year," wrote one *Washington Post* journalist in attendance.

In their private residence, the Yellow Oval Room, the Johnsons preferred a smaller Christmas tree that could be placed on a table. Mrs. Johnson cherished the idea that she was placing the tree in the exact location where President Benjamin Harrison had placed the very first tree to ever grace the White House. Just like the official tree downstairs in the Blue Room, the private family tree was strung with popcorn and cranberries.

Perhaps it was because they split the holiday between Washington and Texas, or maybe it was just the madness of Christmas, but no matter how prepared the Johnsons were, *pandemonium* remained the perfect description of their revelry. Although Mrs. Johnson assured herself each year that she would be more organized the next year, it

ABOVE :: The President and Mrs. Johnson in the Yellow Room in the private residence. Mrs. Johnson made sure their family Christmas tree was placed in the same location as the very first White House Christmas tree.

Mrs. Johnson's desire to beautify America with flowers impacted the Christmas decorations of 1966.

never happened. Eventually, she came to accept the chaos. She wrote in *Redbook* magazine, "Christmas . . . mmm . . . what a lot of laughter, bedlam, crash shopping expeditions and love it conjures up for me."

Some of Lady Bird's most joyful memories resulted from LBJ's impromptu holiday

decisions at the Texas ranch. One Christmas Eve, Lyndon saw a department store Santa walking on the street and paid him twenty-five dollars to come play Santa for the girls. And then there was the Christmas Day that he invited fifty members of the press to tour their house while the holiday dinner got cold, and gave each an ashtray as a Christmas gift. Lyndon once rode a tractor dressed as Santa, and even spent a Christmas Day in the swimming pool, when the temperature hit eighty degrees. The Johnsons went so far as to take a picture holding handwritten signs reading "December 25th" to prove they were swimming on Christmas Day.

In 1967, when President Johnson had been in office for four years, the family decided to spend their first Christmas at the White House. Although Mrs. Johnson bought new ornaments, including silver stars and tiny mirrors, Christmas played second fiddle that year. Lynda Bird Johnson was set to marry Major Charles Robb on December 9. This would be the second wedding the Johnsons celebrated in the White House. Daughter Luci married Patrick John Nugent in 1966 at the Shrine of the Immaculate Conception and had a White House Rose Garden reception.

For Lynda's wedding, 650 guests received the most sought-after invitations of the season.

For Lynda's wedding, 650 guests received the most sought-after invitations of the season.

Only fourteen Senators were invited. Family, foreign dignitaries, and friends populated the list, including Lynda's ex-boyfriend George Hamilton and actress Carol Channing, who

LEFT :: No matter how prepared she tried to be, Lady Bird always had last minute Christmas business! Here, she organizes her Christmas presents at the family ranch in Texas on Christmas Eve, 1965.

ABOVE :: President Johnson walks his daughter Lynda down the aisle at her White House wedding on December 9, 1967.

RIGHT :: Two bridesmaids fix
Lynda's bridal train during the wedding ceremony in the East Room.

shocked Mrs. Johnson by wearing outrageous yellow bloomers that ended
mid-thigh to the wedding.

Decorations for the wedding included
natural greens throughout the house, and
red satin balls on the Grand Staircase. In
the East Room, where the evening wedding ceremony would take place, a raised
altar was erected. Behind the altar a simple
white cross was set against an entire wall of
greens, which was sprinkled with white
Christmas lights. Mrs. Johnson remembered being startled by something peering
out from behind the altar before she realized it was a disguised camera that would
record the event for the nation.

The seven bridesmaids wore red
velvet floor-length dresses with high
necklines and long sleeves, which looked

seasonal as well as stylish. They carried solid red bouquets and wore red velvet bows in their hair. The bride wore a long-sleeved white satin dress with two columns of white rosettes running down the front and around her high-necked collar. On the inside of the dress, embroidered in blue, were the words "Lynda Bird Johnson, December 9, 1967, The White House."

The wedding party proceeded down the Grand Staircase, each bridesmaid escorted by a uniformed marine. Finally, the bride appeared at the top of the staircase holding the arm of her father, President Lyndon Johnson. The wedding march played and the two proceeded to the East Room, where the groom was waiting. Lynda's White House wedding was the embodiment of pomp and circumstance.

The reception was held in a heated tent decorated with red, orange, and pink flowers. Later, the bride threw her bouquet from the staircase landing, and the couple cut the white raisin-and-rum cake with a sword. The Johnsons' dog Yuki crashed the party wearing a red blanket with "Congratulations!" sewn in red sequins.

The greens from Lynda's wedding stayed up for the 1967 holiday season. The red satin ornaments that hung on the staircase were moved to the family's private tree and became part of the family's annual Christmas decorations. That same year, Mrs. Johnson was given a set of Christmas stockings similar to those given to the Kennedy family when John Jr. was born. Each of the Johnsons' stockings

was embellished with a special scene appropriate for the designated member of the family, which now included two sons-in-law and Luci's son, Patrick Lyndon, known as Lyn. Luci's stocking included pictures of the Georgetown University School of Nursing, where she trained as a nurse, one of baby Lyn, and another of wedding rings.

Lady Bird hung these stockings with care in the Yellow Oval Room. They evoked one of her own favorite Christmas memories from

ABOVE :: Lynda Johnson Robb enjoys a quiet December night with her daughter, nephew, and a little friend by the Blue Room tree in 1968.

The red satin ornaments that hung on the staircase were moved to the family's private Christmas tree.

her childhood that she openly shared with the press. It was of her last Christmas with her mother, who had died unexpectedly the following year. Lady Bird was only five at the time. Early Christmas morning, unable to stay in bed any longer, she snuck down the stairs in the darkness and spied her stocking. "There by the fireplace my stocking was filled with nuts and fruit and stick candy—always a part of Christmas in the South—and fireworks to be enjoyed later in the day! Underneath the tree was a little white wicker rocking chair with two fat teddy bears and a beautiful doll."

Mrs. Johnson's growing family became the focal point of Christmas. She wanted to create lasting memories for her children and grandchildren, and so she created Christmas albums. She loved to take an annual Christmas photo of the family, which became known within the family as "The Annual Christmas Horror Show." As if the logistics of getting a Christmas photo with the President of the United States weren't difficult enough, the Johnsons made things even crazier by adding small grandchildren into the mix. Mrs. Johnson shared with *Redbook* magazine memories of the first year they took the Christmas photo with baby Lyn. President Johnson kept getting called away to take phone calls and the baby became cranky, having missed his nap. Frustrated, the President decided to handle the matter himself. "The next few minutes were a side show," the First Lady noted wryly. "Lyndon would poke the bottle in Lyn's mouth, order everyone to 'SMILE,' yank the bottle out of Lyn's mouth, and order the photographer to 'Click.' It went on like this: Bottle to Lyn, Smile, Bottle out of mouth, Howl, click."

While official family photos may have been fraught with chaos, unofficial photos of the Johnson grandchildren in the White House at Christmas are incredibly touching. A series of candid pictures of Lynda with her new baby, Lucy, and her nephew Lyn under the tree in the quiet of the Blue Room, epitomize the magic and wonder of Christmas in the White House.

The last White House Christmas during the Johnson administration was celebrated in

ABOVE :: The official Johnson family Christmas portrait, also known as "The Annual Christmas Horror Show." From left to right: Luci Johnson Nugent; Luci's son, Lyn; Lady Bird; President Johnson; Lynda Johnson Robb; and her daughter, Baby Lucy, on Christmas Eve in 1968.

RIGHT :: The Engelhard crèche is a national historic treasure. Here is a close-up of the angels that soar over the nativity.

Mrs. Johnson loved to take an annual Christmas photo of the family, which became known within the family as "The Annual Christmas Horror Show."

1968. The Johnsons' years in the White House were personally joyous, filled with weddings and the arrival of grandchildren. But President

Johnson's time in office was marred by violence and social upheaval. The Vietnam War continued to claim the lives of American soldiers, and both Martin Luther King Jr. and Bobby Kennedy were assassinated while Johnson was President.

Speaking of her last Christmas in the White House, Lady Bird remembered in her *White House Diary*, "We had an early bedtime, wrapped in that warming sense of family and Christmas and the hope of better years to come." Through trying times for the country, Lady Bird kept her family close and looked to a brighter future.

THE WHITE HOUSE *Crèche*

In 1967 Mrs. Johnson finally secured a permanent crèche, or nativity scene, for the White House. The one lent to Mrs. Kennedy had been returned some years earlier, and the White House had borrowed several nativities since then. That December the White House announced it had received an "exquisite Christmas gift" from Mr. and Mrs. Charles Engelhard of New Jersey. It was an eighteenth-century Italian crèche, complete with "thirty baroque carved figures," each between twelve and eighteen inches high. The crèche had been purchased by the Engelhards in Naples, Italy, from a family who had been collecting nativities for three hundred years.

At the White House, the crèche was originally displayed in the East Room on a fourteen-foot-high baroque stage, crafted by a New York stage designer. The stage was made smaller during the Carter administration, so the crèche could be concealed behind curtains when necessary.

The Engelhard crèche continues to be displayed at the White House. But the traditional Pageant of Peace, the outdoor nativity scene displayed on the Ellipse (the public land adjacent to the White House lawn), has not enjoyed the same longevity. In 1969 a lawsuit was filed stating the Pageant of Peace violated the separation of church and state. The lawsuit dragged on until 1973, when the U.S. Court of Appeals ruled the nativity scene could no longer be displayed on public land. The Engelhard crèche has escaped this fate because it is designated a national treasure and antiquity.

~ *Lady Bird's* ~
CHRISTMAS CRANBERRY SALAD MOLD

Lady Bird Johnson so enjoyed this recipe, she took the time to write a personal message on the recipe card, which is now at the Lyndon Baines Johnson Library and Museum as part of Mrs. Johnson's personal papers. Mrs. Johnson encouraged visitors to try her recipe: "This is decorative and delicious—for the holidays or whenever you serve chicken or turkey."

Ingredients

2 cups cranberries

1¼ cups cold water

1 cup sugar

1 envelope unflavored gelatin

½ cup chopped celery

½ cup chopped nuts

½ teaspoon of salt

* Makes about 6 servings

Tips :: A bit less sugar than the amount listed saves the salad from tasting overly sweet. Although Mrs. Johnson merely lists "nuts" in her list of ingredients, pecans taste fabulous in this recipe. For a modern twist, use wine glasses as your mold. ~

~ STEP *One* Cook cranberries in 1 cup water for 20 minutes. Stir in sugar and cook 5 minutes longer.

~ STEP *Two* Soften gelatin in ¼ cup cold water; add to hot cranberries and stir until dissolved. Set aside to cool.

~ STEP *Three* When mixture begins to thicken, add chopped celery, nuts, and salt. Turn into mold that has been rinsed with cold water. Chill in refrigerator until firm. Unmold on serving plate. Garnish with salad greens if desired.

REPRINTED WITH PERMISSION FROM
THE LYNDON BAINES JOHNSON LIBRARY AND MUSEUM

3

A Season of Gold

PAT NIXON

1969–1974

A SEASON OF GOLD

Pat Nixon

"I want a diamond necklace for Christmas!"

—PAT NIXON, LAUGHING ON SANTA'S LAP IN THE EAST ROOM IN 1969
AS REPORTED IN THE *WASHINGTON POST*

It must have been surreal for the farmer's daughter from California, who was thankful to get nuts, fruit, and a dime in her Depression-era Christmas stocking, to find herself sitting on Santa's lap in the East Room of the White House. Mrs. Nixon never forgot where she came from, or how much work it took to get to 1600 Pennsylvania Avenue. And while she may have joked about wanting a diamond necklace, what she really wanted was to give Americans a priceless Christmas experience.

Pat and Richard Nixon, and their two daughters, Tricia and Julie, were well known to the American people by the time Dick finally won the presidential election of 1968. He had served as Vice President under Dwight "Ike" Eisenhower from 1953 to 1961, and had lost a close race for the presidency to John F. Kennedy in 1960.

November and December of 1968 was a time of celebration for the Nixons for personal as well as political reasons. Just weeks after Nixon was elected President, his daughter Julie married David Eisenhower, Ike's grandson, in a private ceremony (the two met when they were just eight years old at the 1956

Republican National Convention). And for the first time in his family's memory, Richard Nixon did not have to be dragged to the store to go Christmas shopping. He splurged and bought the three women in his life mink coats, which they wore to Christmas Sunday services.

In 1969 Mrs. Nixon chose "State Flower Balls" for her first Christmas theme. The balls were large velvet-and-satin ornaments made by disabled workers in Florida. As their name suggests, the ornaments showcased the flower of each state. Each ornament measured about eight inches, and had a three-dimensional flower attached to it. The tree was trimmed with a long and bushy gold garland, gathered in swags of three. The garland was glitzy, but it only wrapped the tree three times, and left plenty of green showing. The lowest branches actually swept the floor, making a tree skirt unnecessary. Purple and gold balls complemented the state flower balls.

One change Mrs. Nixon made in 1969 was to alter the location of the official tree from the Blue Room to the Grand Foyer. She also brought back twelve free-standing pedestal

PRECEDING SPREAD :: The First Couple admire a snowman made after a December snowfall in 1973. The snowman captured the fancy of the press because he had two faces, one facing the street and one facing the White House. LEFT :: Mrs. Nixon and Julie display a "State Flower Ball" in front of the Official White House Christmas tree, December 13, 1971.

sconces, which Mrs. Kennedy had exiled into storage in 1961. Each was about eight feet tall. In 1969 they were adorned with red candles, wrapped with green roping, and placed at the entrance to the state rooms. The First Lady also introduced a decorating tradition from her own home—she crowned the chandeliers with greens and red bows, and hung blue, red, and gold ornaments from the crystals.

For the first time ever, Mrs. Nixon hung large wreaths, with red bows and candles, in each of the sixteen windows facing Pennsylvania Avenue. This tradition has been carried out by every First Lady since. The second lasting White House Christmas tradition started that year was the gingerbread house. Assistant Pastry Chef Hans Raffert created the two-foot confectionary masterpiece in the White House kitchen. It was done in homage to his German

roots, and appeared to have sprung from the pages of "Hansel and Gretel." The gingerbread house was placed in the State Dining Room and was an immediate hit with both the press and the American public. In fact, so temptingly sweet was the gingerbread house that a marine, complete with braided uniform, stood guard to protect it in case a visitor tried to steal a bite!

One change Mrs. Nixon made in 1969 was to alter the location of the official tree from the Blue Room to the Grand Foyer.

But perhaps the most important Christmas tradition Mrs. Nixon gave to the White House was the Candlelight Christmas Tour. She understood that most Americans were at work during regular hours for touring the

ABOVE :: Mrs. Nixon and Julie peek inside the 1971 gingerbread house.

RIGHT :: The First Couple, with daughter Tricia, in the Grand Foyer of the White House, December 21, 1969.

White House, and so she hit upon the idea of having an evening tour so that more people could enjoy the decorations. The very first

Later that December, Mrs. Nixon and Tricia taped a television special in the Red Room that showcased the Christmas decorations.

candlelight tours were held December 29 and 30, 1969. When possible, real candles were used, and the electric lights were dimmed to create a candlelit atmosphere. Bands from the army, marines, and air force played Christmas carols. Some visitors sang along, and others even danced!

That year Bob Hope performed a rehearsal of his annual "Christmas Show for Servicemen" in the East Room for the First Couple and about three hundred guests. Later that

December, Mrs. Nixon and Tricia taped a television special in the Red Room that showcased the Christmas decorations. The special aired nationally, and was also broadcast to the U.S. troops in Vietnam, who were so far from home that Christmas.

In 1970 the decorations remained much the same as the prior year, with a few exceptions. That Christmas is often referred to as "The Year of the Monroe Fans," because fifty gold foil fans were added to the tree in a tribute to President James Monroe (1817–1825), who liked heavily gilded furnishings and dishes. Earlier that year, Mrs. Nixon had decided to permanently display Monroe's gilded 1817 Parisian china in the Blue Room. The official tree was moved back to the Blue Room, so that the tree, fan ornaments, and china could all be seen in the same place. When the tree arrived from Wisconsin, it already had a small blue satin ball on it. It was a gift from four-year-old Patty Frelk, whose parents had grown the tree. In a bit of foreshadowing, Mrs. Nixon joked the ornament would be in the White House long after she would.

The same Christmas season also saw the creation of several seven-foot poinsettia "trees," which were actually tiered metal stands that held seventy-five red poinsettia plants, arranged to look like one amazing tree. The "trees" were displayed in the East Room.

That year the entire Senate and Congress were invited to the East Room for a Christian worship service. The group planning to attend was so large it had to be split up between two different Sundays. Several hundred guests prayed, sang Christmas hymns, and then attended a reception in the state rooms. This popular event continued on a monthly basis, with different guests, long after Christmas.

Meanwhile, Mrs. Nixon's holiday shopping caused quite a commotion. Word spread throughout the city when she and a friend went to D.J. Pampillonia and Sons. Pampillonia claimed to be the "Court Jeweler to Washington VIPs," with good reason—Jackie, Ethel, and Joan Kennedy were all customers. The First Lady splurged, buying Trisha and Julie jeweled earrings and the President a pair of jeweled cuff links. The story of the President's Christmas present was leaked to the newspapers. When asked if she was upset that her Christmas surprise for her husband was spoiled, the First Lady laughingly told the *Washington Post*

that her secret was still safe "because Dick never reads the women's pages."

Another gift that season also caused an uproar. It was from the King himself—Elvis Presley. On December 20, Elvis came to the White House and brought President Nixon an early Christmas present—a Colt .45! Elvis also had an idea for the President: He wanted to be deputized a federal narcotics agent and use his

On December 20, Elvis came to the White House and brought President Nixon an early Christmas present— a Colt .45!

fame to encourage the youth of America to support President Nixon's war on drugs. Hoping to be of service to his country, Elvis said in a letter to the President, "First and foremost I am an entertainer, but all I need is the federal

RIGHT :: Mrs. Nixon loved to decorate the White House chandeliers, but this look drew criticism from the public. In the background is the staircase to the family's private residence.

credentials." That day his ambitions were thwarted, and it seems all he got was an autographed picture with President Nixon.

"Gold Foil Angels" was the theme in 1971, and the official tree became even glitzier. The First Lady wanted to use many of the decorations from the year before, but she also wanted "a new wrinkle" to keep it interesting. She turned to Saks Fifth Avenue vice president Henry Callahan, who had helped decorate the White House in the past. In a letter, Mr. Callahan suggested using rose-colored lights. The idea was not well received, and someone, most likely Mrs. Nixon or her social secretary, Lucy Winchester, wrote a bold, definite "NO!!" on the letter next to Mr. Callahan's idea. Another of his suggestions, which was much better received, was the idea to specially commission larger bronze angels to complement the gold

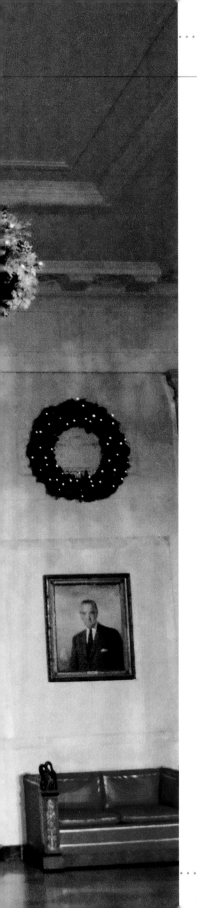

foil ones. But just days before the decorations were to go up, the bronze angels were destroyed during the shipping process. Mr. Callahan vowed to never send anything else that could be so easily damaged.

In a new twist, narrow green topiary Christmas trees sat atop the sconces, and were trimmed with gold balls.

In addition to the angel ornamentation, both intact and destroyed, the 1971 Yule decor once again included the pedestal sconces and the greens-covered chandeliers. In a new twist, narrow green topiary Christmas trees sat atop the sconces, and were trimmed with gold balls. And instead of a single crown of greens, each chandelier received three tiers of holly, giving them a ringed effect. (Mrs. Nixon later noted the tiers proved unpopular, and it was not repeated.) Natural roping draped the Cross Hall columns, extending halfway down. All the mantels were done in red poinsettias and miniature creeping ivy, which Mrs. Nixon liked because the ivy hid the poinsettias' pots.

That year Yogi Bear, Boo-Boo Bear, and Bullwinkle all made a trip to the East Room to perform for the Diplomatic Children's Party. Mrs. Nixon happily attended, as she had in the past. Over five hundred children from Embassy Row came, and all were in the dress of their native country, which was a recent custom at the party. When they finished watching the show, the children sang Mrs. Nixon her favorite Christmas carol—"Rudolph the Red-Nosed Reindeer."

Later that week, a *Washington Post* reporter asked Mrs. Nixon how she was doing with her Christmas shopping, and she laughed, "Don't you remember, I did my shopping with Julie at Sears!" In fact, she had. The trip to Sears was a well-publicized PR event, created because Sears was supporting the second phase of the President's controversial economic plan. According to the plan, a board of economic advisers would control prices and wages in an attempt to thwart growing inflation.

It's been noted that Mrs. Nixon wanted to give as many Americans as possible a chance to experience Christmas in the White House. She achieved this not only through the candlelight tours, but also by making the White House accessible to the handicapped. It was Mrs. Nixon who had the first ramps installed, and she also was responsible for designing Christmas tours for visitors who were deaf or blind.

During a visit to the Junior School for the Blind in Los Angeles, Mrs. Nixon had invited the students to come visit her sometime at the White House. In 1971 enough private donations had been raised to send the students to DC. When they finished the Christmas tour Mrs. Nixon had implemented, they serenaded her with the song "Climb Every Mountain." Mrs. Nixon then had them climb the steps to the Lincoln Bedroom, where the children piled on top of each other on the bed! It was a tour like no other. In her biography, *Pat Nixon: The Untold Story,* Mrs. Nixon shared one student's impression:

> ⌒ I'm on cloud ninety. Do you know about nine? I'm way above that. I'd be on cloud nine hundred, if I could stand the altitude! ⌒

Christmas Eve 1971 came to a cozy end with the Nixons, their two daughters, and both sons-in-law exchanging gifts in the White House private residence. The Nixons' upcoming trip to China had sparked lively discussion, as did Julie's gift to her father of *The Feminine Mystique,* by Betty Friedan. As the family dogs King, Timahoe, Pusha, and Vicky played with their annual doggie stockings, David Eisenhower ribbed his father-in-law by giving him a recording of dogs barking Christmas carols. All things considered, the Nixon family had a very normal Christmas.

Mrs. Nixon had sent most of the staff home to enjoy the holiday, and the Nixons, like millions of people across America, ate leftovers and watched football on TV.

All the green finery—the roping, swags, and greens on the mantels and in the chandeliers—were decorated with artificial fruit.

In 1972 the holiday mood at the White House was definitely jolly. The President had been reelected by an unprecedented landslide, which he attributed to the Silent Majority, people who did not demonstrate against the Vietnam War and were not members of the counterculture. Few, if anyone, cared about the past summer's break-in at the Watergate office complex.

The Christmas theme was "Nature's Bounty," inspired by a lush still life painting of fruit and flowers by the German-born American artist Severin Roesen. All the green finery—the roping, swags, and greens on the mantels and in the chandeliers—were decorated with artificial fruit instead of ornaments. In addition, three thousand pastel satin balls and 150 gold stars were added to the state flower balls on the big Christmas tree. The columns in the Cross Hall were almost entirely covered in red velvet.

That year the invitation list for the Diplomatic Children's Party swelled to a thousand. There was snow on the ground, and Julie thought the children would love a snowman. One was made, complete with hands fashioned

RIGHT :: The Nixon family and their beloved dogs during an interview in the Yellow Room.

into the President's signature victory sign. The snowman faced Pennsylvania Avenue. Two White House social aides came by and, not realizing the snowman represented the President, thought it would be cute for the diplomatic children to see a smiling snowman as they entered the party from the opposite direction. They put a second face on the snowman. An eagle-eyed photographer from *Time* magazine noted the irony of the two-faced presidential snowman and snapped away. It ran in the next issue.

The party itself was a huge success, with special guests from the *New Zoo Revue*, a popular children's TV show with music. Although stars like Henrietta Hippo and Freddie the Frog mingled in the East Room, it was Mrs. Nixon's autograph that every child wanted! At the close of the party, at the top of their lungs,

the children shouted, "MERRY CHRIST-MAS, MRS. NIXON!"

Christmas 1973 was the year of the "Gold Tree Honoring James Monroe." Although the tree was again done in gold and hung with the state flower balls, it was more delicate this time. The bushy garland was replaced by dainty strings of gold beads. The red velvet was removed from the columns in the Cross Hall and was replaced with a shimmery gold material. Arches of greenery were built between the columns, and dotted with gold balls.

The 1973 Christmas tree was dressed in dainty strands of gold beads and hung with state flower balls.

As usual, a large party was held for the diplomats' children, and this time *Sesame Street* characters joined Mrs. Nixon in championing

ABOVE :: Always an innovator with decorations, Mrs. Nixon covered the Cross Hall columns in a shimmering gold material and built arches of greens in the Grand Lobby, 1973.

RIGHT :: Mrs. Nixon and the President pose in front of the Presidential Seal at Camp David, Christmas 1971.

one of her favorite causes: the Right to Read Literacy Program. The party was so raucous that a social aide had to be assigned to protect Big Bird's bottom from reaching hands trying to pluck his feathers.

It's uncertain if either President or Mrs. Nixon suspected that 1973 would be their last Christmas in the White House. The great highs they had experienced all seemed to have been overshadowed by the dark stain of Watergate. Even the mink coats the President happily gave his wife and daughters for Christmas in 1968 no longer represented joy. The Special Prosecutor's Office had included the mink coats, and their insurance policies, in the ongoing investigation of the Nixon administration. As history continues to evaluate the presidency of Richard Nixon, one thing is clear: President Nixon may have opened up foreign relations with China, but it was Mrs. Nixon who opened up the White House at Christmas to the American people, including the working class and the disabled.

THE NATION'S *Ideal* HOUSEWIFE

In December 1957, when Pat Nixon was Second Lady, over a million people cast votes in a Homemakers Forum contest, choosing Pat as "the Nation's Ideal Housewife." And just what did the Nation's Ideal Housewife do for the holidays? She allowed her daughters to Christmas shop with a weekly allowance of fifty cents (minus dues for Girl Scouts and contributions for Sunday school), bought her husband ties and thick socks, hung gifts of mittens on a revolving musical tree, and like mothers all over the country, became nostalgic when she looked at her growing children. Of Tricia she once said, "I'm so glad she wants a doll, for when she stops wanting a doll, I'll be sorry."

Pat Nixon's

ELEGANT CHANDELIER RINGED WITH GREENS

I couldn't wait to try Mrs. Nixon's idea to decorate the chandelier (my version pictured left). Long before she got to the White House, Mrs. Nixon decorated the chandelier for Christmas in her own house. She experimented with different looks over the years. In the beginning, she merely hung blue and red balls from her chandelier. Later, when she was First Lady, Mrs. Nixon used natural greens to create a dense green ring around the White House chandeliers.

Supplies

Scissors or sharp knife for cutting floral wire

Greens, preferably boxwood if you have a crystal chandelier, or evergreen branches (see Tip)

Green floral wire

Festive bows (optional)

Ornaments (optional)

Tip :: The amount of greenery you will need will depend on the size of your chandelier and your personal preference. Mrs. Nixon liked to stuff the chandelier, creating a thick, dense ring.

STEP *One* If you are working with a traditional crystal hanging chandelier, and a metal ring is part of the fixture's support structure, take the greens and gently slide them over the metal ring until you cover it, working your way completely around its circumference. If your chandelier does not have this type of support structure, and it has several arms, you will need to create a ring to place over the arms. To do this, make a rope of greens using green floral wire and greens. Start by using your floral wire to connect individual pieces of greens to each other, creating a rope of greens. Stop when you have enough to circle the chandelier. This will be a less structured ring. Drape the roping over the arms, attaching the two ends to each other with floral wire. Use floral wire to secure your roping to the fixture as needed.

STEP *Two* If you wish, attach a festive bow to either the top or the bottom of the chandelier. Mrs. Nixon also liked to attach ornaments, which you may want to try.

4

A Homespun Christmas

BETTY FORD

1974–1977

A HOMESPUN CHRISTMAS

Betty Ford

In the Blue Room, Jerry pointed to the magnificent tree that stretched clear to the ceiling and told the thousand guests—from the Hill, the Cabinet, the senior White House staff—that he and the Christmas tree, also from Michigan, had a lot in common. "A few months ago neither one of us expected to be in the White House."

—BETTY FORD, RECALLING THE WORDS OF HER HUSBAND
FROM *THE TIMES OF MY LIFE*

Perhaps no one was as surprised as Gerald and Betty Ford that they were President and First Lady following the resignation of Richard Nixon. In the aftermath of Watergate, the White House was in need of a media makeover, and Mrs. Ford rose to the task. Her unexpected role as First Lady would be one of many challenges she would face in life, including a very public battle with breast cancer and a lifelong struggle with alcoholism, which led to her most lasting legacy, the Betty Ford Center in Rancho Mirage, California.

Mrs. Ford's immediate goal in the fall of 1974 was to strike a distinctly different tone than her predecessor's, and a good place to start was with Christmas. She proposed the White House adopt the Ford family's traditions, which were based on creativity, love, and above all, thriftiness. The Accidental

President had met Betty Bloomer, a former professional dancer who studied with Martha Graham, when he was already a congressman. They had four children—Mike, Steven, Jack, and Susan, though only teenage Susan lived in the White House with her parents. The Fords always had wonderful Christmas celebrations. Growing up, Susan baked the neighbors cookies and the boys were in charge of decorating the outside of the house with paper wreaths and spray snow. Mrs. Ford loved her children's Christmas efforts, despite their imperfect nature. She insisted her children follow one mandatory rule at Christmas: no more than a dollar could be spent on a present.

Mrs. Ford kept her family's approach in mind when she chose "Patchwork Christmas" as her 1974 theme. According to her staff, a patchwork Christmas was as easy and convenient as

PRECEDING PAGE :: Mrs. Ford holds the press preview of the calico Christmas decorations on December 10, 1974. RIGHT :: Mrs. Ford and her daughter, Susan, make homemade Christmas ornaments for Christmas 1975. This photo was included as part of a cover story in *Parade* magazine.

RIGHT :: A 1975 Christmas tree, one of several hung with handmade ornaments, is placed in front of a window in the West Sitting Hall.

peeking in your sewing basket and using whatever you have at hand. The official press release read:

> ⌒ Warmth, humility, and endearing simplicity are the cornerstones for the White House Christmas Decor this year. The Fords have arrived and with them blow the winds of Hometown America. Suddenly, the usually opulent White House has become a home in which any American would feel comfortable this Christmas. ⌒

But it wasn't just family tradition and the need to make a public break from the Nixon administration that inspired Mrs. Ford's choice of a "Patchwork Christmas." It was a "Patchwork Christmas" because it had to be. The country was in a horrible recession, with long gas lines the norm at the few stations that actually had

gas to sell. President Ford declared inflation "Public Enemy Number One" and had buttons made that read "WIN!" an acronym for "Whip Inflation Now!" But the buttons and the campaign were universally mocked for their ineffectuality. Mrs. Ford, acutely aware of the administration's image, chose her Christmas theme accordingly.

She dismissed the Saks Fifth Avenue designer who had worked with the Nixons, and chose not to use any of the ornaments Mrs. Nixon left behind. Mrs. Ford eschewed everything that seemed extravagant, including gold and tinsel. She wanted a Christmas visit to the White House not to feel like a tour of a stately mansion, but rather, like a Christmas visit to Grandma's house. Handcrafted decorations and an aura of thriftiness would replace the glitter of earlier years.

The patchwork theme was used in both the state rooms and the Fords' private living quarters. Quilting, including informal patchwork designs, appealed to Mrs. Ford because they epitomized the motto "Waste not, want not." Mrs. Ford loved the idea of quilting so much that she even considered having a Christmas quilting bee at the White House. Susan poked gentle fun at her mother's decorating passions, and went so far as to create a patchwork ornament that read "Betty Ford in '74."

An American-made, pastel-blue calico fabric was chosen to coordinate the tree's decorations with the Blue Room. Three hundred feet of garland and eighteen oversized

bows were made from the fabric and hung from the tree. Appalachian crafters and New York quilters made 550 patchwork ornaments in the shapes of balls, pentagons, and lanterns. The tree was laden with 600 tiny mirrors, homemade spice sachets of cinnamon and nutmeg, tiny Cherokee baskets filled with nuts or gumdrops, and ribbon candy. Carved wooden toys in the shapes of animals were hung from the tree, and were later given to underprivileged children as Christmas presents.

Remembering Christmas 1974, Mrs. Ford wrote, "The decorations were fabulous: the State Floor [state rooms] became a fairyland." A quilt wrapped the base of the tree, and both natural and calico wreaths were hung about the house. Red candles replaced the normal white candles in candelabras, and poinsettias grown in the White House green-

house were placed throughout the state rooms. Ten angels with trumpets, two of which were life-size, were made from aluminum and sprayed with gold paint. Even these were trimmed with calico fabric. Mrs. Ford went as far as to suggest Christmas presents could be wrapped in fabric.

The star of the '74 "Patchwork Christmas" was clearly the tree, but the day it arrived, some other celebrities were visiting the White House

ABOVE :: This is the colorful sign that accompanied the official Christmas tree when it arrived in 1974.

Handcrafted decorations and an aura of thriftiness would replace the glitter of earlier years.

and distracted Mrs. Ford. The Harlem Globetrotters were waiting just outside the Oval Office to meet the President when Mrs. Ford spotted the famed Trotter Meadowlark Lemon. She asked him to teach her to play

basketball, and before she knew it, they were tossing the basketball around the White House. They didn't realize how noisy they were until the President sent Defense secretary Donald Rumsfeld "with word," Mrs. Ford wrote later in her memoir, "that the President said there was too much noise in the outer office, and whoever was carrying on, would they please stop. Cease. Desist from their activities."

Once the decorating was done, Mrs. Ford remembered, "The Christmas parties started and I didn't think they'd ever stop." As was customary, there were parties at children's hospitals, as well as the Diplomatic Children's Party and the Residence Staff Party. The Fords only made a brief appearance at the Christmas Press Party, as it was scheduled at the same time as the swearing-in of Nelson

Rockefeller as Vice President. When the First Couple returned to the White House at eleven in the evening, they were shocked to find the party, slated to end at nine, still in full swing! But the most anticipated party of the season was the Congressional Christmas Ball, a White House tradition that Mrs. Ford reinstated. Inspired by the beauty of the

Mrs. Ford had spent sixteen hundred dollars at a time when the recession was crippling the country.

White House Christmas decorations, Mrs. Ford declared the state rooms a perfect setting for a black tie affair.

For all the effort that went into Mrs. Ford's thrifty "Patchwork Christmas," in the end it was more expensive than the Christmas decorations of Mrs. Kennedy, Mrs. Johnson,

RIGHT :: Mrs. Ford so loved homemade Christmas ornaments, she even provided instructions for some of her favorites! Here are the actual instructions for a Clothespin Cardinal, pictured with a Clothespin Cardinal made by volunteers at the Gerald Ford Presidential Library for Christmas 2010.

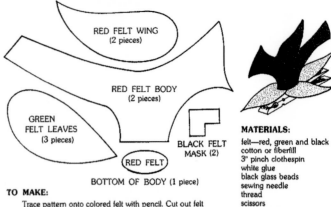

CLOTHESPIN CARDINAL

RED FELT WING
(2 pieces)

RED FELT BODY
(2 pieces)

GREEN
FELT LEAVES
(3 pieces)

BLACK FELT
MASK (2)

RED FELT

BOTTOM OF BODY (1 piece)

MATERIALS:
felt—red, green and black
cotton or fiberfill
3″ pinch clothespin
white glue
black glass beads
sewing needle
thread
scissors
1″ dressmaker's straight pins
pencil

TO MAKE:

Trace pattern onto colored felt with pencil. Cut out felt pieces. Assemble pieces into body shape; sew around edges of cardinal's body leaving 1″ space at bottom open. Stuff bird with cotton or fiberfill; close 1″ opening. Sew red felt base onto bottom of bird. Glue three green felt leaves to top of 3″ pinch clothespin. Glue stuffed bird to top of leaves. Glue or sew black glass beads on for eyes, or use tiny squares of black felt for eyes. Attach clothespin to tree.

THE PRESIDENT AND I WISH YOU MERRY CHRISTMAS

Betty Ford

and Mrs. Nixon! Mrs. Ford had spent sixteen hundred dollars at a time when the recession was crippling the country. It was a PR disaster. Mrs. Ford herself was shocked that she'd spent so much. Although the money went mostly to craft groups and women's cooperatives, she was widely criticized. She defended herself, saying that the Christmas efforts put people back to work, and she made certain the bills were paid from her own residence housekeeping budget.

In 1975 Mrs. Ford didn't make the same mistake. A "Children's Christmas" was paid for by the Colonial Williamsburg Foundation and the Abby Aldrich Rockefeller Folk Art Collection. The Abby Aldrich collection championed American artists without formal training. The staff

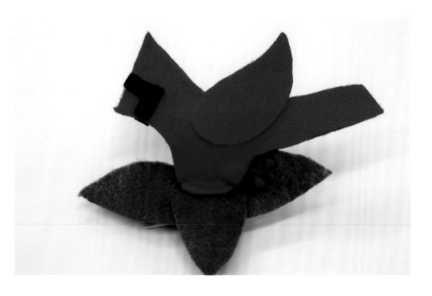

at Abby Aldrich coordinated the decorations and lent antique toys, which were used throughout the house.

The marching orders for 1975 were the same as 1974: no sequins, no glitter, no foil. The tree would be decorated with American crafts, using materials like yarn, wire, corn husks, patchwork animals, clothespins, and straw. Mrs. Ford and her daughter, Susan, did a photo spread and story with *Parade* magazine showing how such ornaments could be made. The White House even provided step-by-step directions: you simply had to write a letter to Mrs. Ford care of the White House, with "Christmas Ornament Instruction" written in the address line. With time and Mrs. Ford's guidance, you could make a corn husk doll, nut person, soap snowflake, cookie cutter tree toy, paper silhouette, or clothespin cardinal. Mrs. Ford herself was very fond of stringing popcorn and sewing felt ornaments in the shape of animals. To Mrs. Johnson's traditional gingerbread ornaments, Mrs. Ford added an Italian cookie called the pizzelle, which is a thin wafer in the shape of a snowflake. She was known to steal a cookie right off the tree for a snack.

The "Children's Christmas" had several elements beyond the tree. Ten folk art portraits of children, by different artists, hung in the Blue Room. A large camel and giraffe from an antique carousel stood on either side of the doorway to the room. An antique Santa, on loan from the Smithsonian, peered over the Grand Staircase landing. Of course, there were natural greens and a gingerbread house.

ABOVE :: Santa and Mrs. Claus decorations sit atop a quilt on the State Floor, Christmas 1974.

That year a new tradition was started—the cranberry tree. It harkened back to Colonial America, and as its name suggests, it was covered in fresh cranberries. The cranberries were applied to a topiary cone, which stood about two feet tall. When completed, it was placed as a decoration in the Red Room. It's a long-held secret that two cranberry trees are made each

The 1975 tree was decorated with American crafts, using materials like yarn, wire, corn husks, patchwork animals, clothespins, and straw.

season. One is displayed until it begins to spoil, and then the second emerges fresh from refrigeration, and no one is the wiser.

Mrs. Ford's preparations were not limited to ornaments and decorations that holiday season. She also taped an appearance on *The*

RIGHT :: Mrs. Ford hangs ornaments on the 1976 Blue Room tree at
the press preview of the decorations.

FAR RIGHT :: First Lady Betty
Ford and daughter, Susan, pose with
White House favorites, Santa and
Big Bird!

Mary Tyler Moore Show, which aired right after
Christmas. Although Mrs. Ford was not
expecting to be paid, the Screen Actors Guild
insisted, and the First Lady was issued a check
for $172.50, which she donated to an organi-
zation that bought Christmas presents for
underprivileged children.

For Christmas 1976, the year of the
nation's Bicentennial, Mrs. Ford chose the
theme "America Is Love." It was a phrase she
was fond of using to describe her feelings for
our country: "America is love! America is all of
us." Christmas 1976 was the Fords' last in the
White House because Gerald Ford had lost the
presidential election to Jimmy Carter that
November. Still, it was Christmas and it was
the Bicentennial. Plans made that fall were put
into action: Big red velvet bows accented the
greens, and the Blue Room tree was covered in

2,500 handmade flowers, representing all fifty states. The flowers were made of a variety of materials: silk, metal, shells, felt, bamboo, glass, seeds, and beads. A nosegay of flowers crowned the tree's top, and gifts wrapped in red, white, and blue encircled the base. Patriotic treasures dotted the rooms, including a white hand-carved dove with an olive branch and two handmade Bicentennial dolls—Betsy Ross and Paul Revere.

As her days as First Lady came to a close, Mrs. Ford reflected on the Christmas memories she had collected on her road to the White House, including the remembrances of Grandma Ford knitting a miniature stocking for Susan's Tiny Tears doll and the tree skirt made from Jerry's campaign memorabilia. To end 1976, Betty Ford packed up her family and headed to Vail, Colorado, a favorite Christmas vacation destination. It was the last time they had to rent a home spacious enough to house not only their family but also a large Secret Service detail. Mrs. Ford told *Parade* magazine that the Fords exchanged gifts and had a quick breakfast on Christmas morning. And like Christmases in the past, immediately after breakfast, "the kids are off to the slopes, the President being the oldest boy of all, leading the way."

And so Jerry Ford spent Christmas Day 1976 on skis. This same wintery scene repeated itself for many years, until President Ford grew too old to ski. He passed away on December 26, 2006, having enjoyed ninety-three Christmas seasons, three of which were in the White House.

Betty's Ode to *Big Bird*

Mrs. Nixon's friend Big Bird made a return visit to the East Room to meet Mrs. Ford and entertain schoolchildren during the Christmas season of 1976. Mrs. Ford revealed that she had written America's favorite yellow bird a poem! Below is the actual poem Mrs. Ford wrote and recited on December 14, 1976:

CHRISTMAS IN OUR LAND
IS FULL OF GOOD CHEER
WITH STORIES OF SANTA
AND HIS MANY REINDEER

HERE AT THE WHITE HOUSE
IT MAKES US QUITE JOLLY
TO HAVE YOU COME JOIN US
FOR SOME HOLIDAY FOLLY

AND BECAUSE YOU'RE SO SPECIAL
WE ASKED THE BIG BIRD
TO TELL US SOME STORIES
WE NEVER HAVE HEARD

AND WE HOPE YOU'LL ENJOY
OUR BIG FUNNY TREAT
WITH BIG BIRD AND FRIENDS
FROM SESAME STREET.

Betty Ford's
CRANBERRY TREE

I knew Mrs. Ford's Cranberry Tree would be the perfect centerpiece for any holiday table. Inspired by the original, I created the tree pictured left. Mrs. Ford made a cranberry tree part of the White House decorations in 1975. It stands a foot and a half tall and makes a stunning table-top decoration. The tree will look its best for about two weeks. Consider making two trees at once, storing one in the refrigerator, and replacing the first when the berries no longer look fresh.

Supplies

Styrofoam cone, about 1½ feet tall (available at craft stores)

Floral moss

Floral wire or 1¹⁄₁₆-inch straight pins, depending on preference

3 (1-pound) bags fresh cranberries (see Tips)

White glue

Clear acrylic lacquer spray

Red Spray paint (optional; see Tips)

Tips :: Dark cranberries produce the richest-looking tree. Do not use frozen cranberries. They are quite messy when they thaw. For time-saving shortcuts, you can use straight pins instead of floral wire and paint the cone with red spray paint, instead of using glue and floral moss. The paint dries faster.

STEP *One* To make the tree according to the White House method: Glue floral moss to the entire cone. Cut the floral wire into 1-inch strips. Push the wire through the center of a cranberry, dip it in glue, and push it into the cone. Repeat until the cone is covered. Spray with acrylic lacquer to preserve shelf life.

STEP *Two* Place the cranberry tree on a festive plate or surround it with holiday greens at the base.

5

A Christmas of Restraint

ROSALYNN CARTER

1977–1981

A CHRISTMAS OF RESTRAINT
Rosalynn Carter

"I don't know how she confused chain saw with electric train, which is what Amy really wanted, but the story spread and chain saws began arriving at the White House, even one that was red, white, and blue with stars on it."

—ROSALYNN CARTER • FROM *FIRST LADY FROM PLAINS*

It was 1977, and a young friend of Amy Carter had mistakenly told a reporter that the First Daughter wanted a chain saw for Christmas. It was a nod to the down-home nature of the First Family that the country actually believed a little girl could want a chain saw. Suddenly the White House was abuzz with portable power saws, which were promptly sent back with good wishes to the gift givers.

The fact that there was now a youngster in the White House, the first one since the Kennedy children, influenced the White House Christmas planning. A mere ten years old for her first White House Christmas, Amy was the perfect age to be dazzled by holiday magic. In the coming years, special events and shows would be planned with Amy in mind. The Carters also had three sons, and two of them, Chip and Jeff, also moved into the White House. Their eldest son, Jack, was already married when his father was elected President.

In 1977 prices skyrocketed as inflation hit 18 percent, and jobs disappeared. Add a fuel shortage, and no one had money for extravagant holiday spending, not even the President. The oil shortage would mean a lower thermostat setting and more sweaters at the White House, even at Christmas. A humorous Christmas portrait shows the entire family wearing winter hats indoors.

As a couple, the Carters shared thoughts and responsibilities, and this way of doing things extended to Christmas. Insiders noted that the President was almost as involved as Mrs. Carter in the decorating decisions.

Cognizant of the grim economic backdrop, Mrs. Carter proceeded with the Christmas model she had used as First Lady of Georgia. She turned off extra lights and decorated with natural ornamentation like pinecones and strung popcorn. Christmas 1977 would be a simple Georgia Christmas at the White House. The theme was a "Classic American Christmas with Handmade Crafts," but it is more commonly known by

PRECEDING SPREAD :: Mrs. Carter holds an ornament on the 1978 "Antique Toys" Christmas tree.
LEFT :: The Carters' first White House Christmas portrait, with daughter, Amy, in 1977.

its unofficial name, "Milk Pods and Egg-shells." This name is a reference to the natural materials used to craft the ornaments. The Georgia Flower Ladies, a garden club whose members had helped Mrs. Carter decorate Georgia's governor's mansion, traveled to Washington, DC, to help decorate the White House. The National Association for Retarded Citizens, whose cause the First Lady champi-oned, was also called upon to help. Mentally disabled citizens of all ages crafted fifteen hundred ornaments for the tree out of milk pods and eggshells. Upside-down birthday hats were given lace handles and filled with peanuts in a humorous tribute to the Presi-dent's former occupation as a peanut farmer. Amy hung a homemade ornament of her own on the tree—a big green worm fashioned from pipe cleaners.

A performance of *The Littlest Clown* delighted not only Amy but also the entire au-dience at the Diplomatic Children's Party. The young guests were given a small bag of pep-permints as a gift, and a menu of cookies and punch was served.

Prudent with public funds, Mrs. Carter was known for her modest menus, and many events offered no refreshments at all. Still, al-most every White House event offered music.

Mentally disabled citizens of all ages crafted fifteen hundred ornaments.

By inviting choirs to sing Christmas carols at holiday events, Mrs. Carter hit on a way to enliven them without spending additional money. Choirs from around the country made the trip to the White House, including the

ABOVE :: The extended Carter family don hats in their Christmas picture to support of the Presi-dent's appeal to conserve energy.

RIGHT :: The Carter family opens presents at home in Plains, Georgia, 1978.

Strong Museum in New York loaned the White House twenty-five hundred antique toys. The larger ones decorated the state rooms, while hundreds of miniature toys hung on the Blue Room tree. A large dollhouse sat at the base, and the job of decorating it fell to a very special volunteer: eleven-year-old Amy.

By December 1979, the United States was in the throes of the Iranian hostage crisis. This crisis, probably more than any other event during Carter's administration, impacted the First Family at Christmas. In her autobiography, *First Lady from Plains*, Mrs. Carter remembers the night her husband and Amy went to the Ellipse to light the National Christmas Tree:

Singing Angels from Ohio, the Trinity Boys Choir from Pennsylvania, and the Youth Chorale from the DC public schools.

In 1977 the Broadway play *Annie* was the love of all young girls, and a shortened Christmas version was performed in the East Room at the Residence Staff Party. The menu for this

⌐ After Jimmy delivered a somber Christmas message to the nation, Amy pulled the switch to turn on the Christmas lights. The crowds gasped as the tree remained dark, lit only by a large star on top. ⌐

Although they were agonizing over the hostages, the Carters felt it would be wise to continue with the traditions of the holiday season.

party included sliced turkey and ham and assorted cold appetizers. Santa made an appearance, and as was usual that holiday season, peppermints were given out.

The following year, Christmas 1978, the theme "Antique Toys" was clearly chosen with Amy in mind. The Margaret Woodbury

The President explained the tree would remain dark until the fifty hostages were brought home. Fifty smaller trees, one for each hostage, also lined the Ellipse. Like the big tree, the smaller trees also only had a single light on top.

Although they were agonizing over the hostages, the Carters felt it would be wise to continue with the traditions of the holiday season. They did not want to disappoint those for whom Christmas at the White House meant so much. But more importantly, they did not

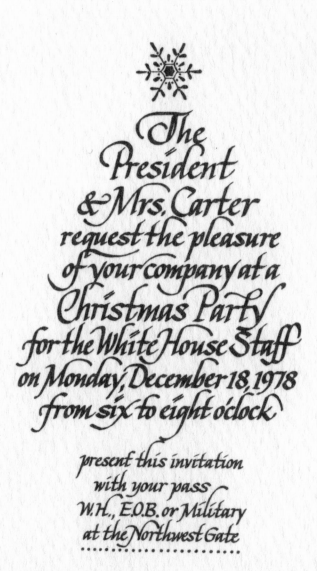

The
President
& Mrs. Carter
request the pleasure
of your company at a
Christmas Party
for the White House Staff
on Monday, December 18, 1978
from six to eight o'clock

present this invitation
with your pass
W.H., E.O.B. or Military
at the Northwest Gate

want to give more power to the Iranian militants who were holding American citizens hostage by canceling Christmas. For this important reason, Christmas would be celebrated. Events like the Congressional Christmas Ball and the candlelight tours of the White House went on as planned.

The 1979 theme was "American Folk Art of the Colonial Period." Students at the Corcoran School of Art (now the Corcoran College of Art and Design), affiliated with the largest private museum in Washington, DC, created ornaments out of needlework, ceramic, and wood. A blue Christmas ball was the unifying ornament on the tree, while under the tree there were large artistic clay ornaments wrapped in clear plastic boxes tied with bows.

Although initial plans called for only white poinsettias and greens to complement the tree, more decorations were added, which led to a humorous blunder. It started simply. Red poinsettias were added to the white, and red felt bows were attached to the wreaths. A few strands of green and red "Italian lights" were used, and the Cross Hall columns were wrapped in green roping.

And then someone had the idea of adding fresh apples. They were simple and wholesome and they spoke of the earth and farming, which was perfect for a White House headed by a former farmer.

Pyramids of apples and bowls filled with still more apples were arranged in the state rooms. What happened next should have been anticipated: The apples began to rot. A fruit fly invasion followed, and eventually all the decorations had to be taken apart and redone. Needless to say, artificial apples were purchased the second time around. That same year, the East Room saw performances of *Snow White* and *Babar the Elephant*, and Mel Torme sang at the White House Residence Staff Party.

The plan that Christmas was for the First Family to spend Christmas Day at Camp David, but as the date drew closer, the Carters realized it would be a very small celebration, with just the President, the First Lady, and Amy. They contemplated a lonely Christmas, when Amy had an idea. Why not invite the White House residence staff and their families to join them? Many had never been to Camp David during their years of service. So two buses filled with residence staff turned the prospect of a solitary Christmas into a

merry holiday. Despite the fun, the plight of the hostages could not be forgotten. Mrs. Carter longed for their return. She wrote in her autobiography, "I had thought we just might have the most wonderful Christmas present in the world—I thought the hostages might come home." It was not to be.

Christmas 1980 was the Carters' last one in the White House, as the President had

Large porcelain dolls hung from parasols on the 1980 tree.

been defeated by Ronald Reagan in his bid for reelection that November. The theme was an "Old-Fashioned Victorian Christmas." The Blue Room tree was done in muted mauves and pinks. Large porcelain dolls hung from parasols on the tree, as did even larger

RIGHT :: The Carters welcome Olympian Peggy Fleming and her ice skating troupe to the White House Winter Festival in 1980.

FAR RIGHT :: Mrs. Carter's decorations were often as simple as colored table clothes adorned with natural greenery.

Victorian puppets. Artificial flowers decorated the tree: single roses, small bouquets, and large ball ornaments completely covered in faux flowers. There were also ornaments made from pale-colored fabrics and adorned with lace, and plain pink and mauve balls. Large rose-colored tassels hung on the tree. There was a dollhouse at the base, surrounded by Victorian dolls in a variety of sizes, as well as hatboxes, lace parasols, and Victorian nosegays.

While the inside of the White House looked peaceful and old-fashioned, the celebrations going on outside were spectacular, complete with manufactured snow and an ice rink. There was a Winter Lawn Festival, whose first event was a snowman-making contest, with President Carter acting as the judge. It was followed by two ice-skating shows starring the Olympic gold medalist Peggy Fleming.

A White House memo advised, "Guests should wear snow clothes." Two thousand guests, seated in chairs rather than bleachers, enjoyed each show. The menu was all-American and included hot dogs with rolls, roasted chestnuts, popcorn, hot chocolate, and spiced cider.

The next day, the Carters returned to their home in Plains, Georgia, and in the President's diary it was recorded that from 3:58 until 6:30 p.m., "the President and Amy Carter cut a Christmas tree." Throughout their four years in the White House, the Carters had held onto a simple life, and they were returning to just that.

Mrs. Carter's dream that the hostages would be freed for Christmas 1979 remained unfulfilled again in 1980. They weren't released until January 1981 when President Reagan made his inaugural speech on the steps of the Capitol. As they took their very last Air Force One flight back to Georgia, the Carters got the joyous news they had been waiting for so long: The hostages were safe and on their way home.

COOKIES AND PUNCH AND
Patchwork

Do you think cookies and punch make a fitting White House treat? If you were a guest of Mrs. Carter, this is probably what you were served. Cookies and punch played a surprisingly prominent role in Mrs. Carter's entertainment. It was the obligatory menu at almost every event. The cookies-and-punch menu did expand to include other food and drink, depending on the importance of the event. For example, guarding the President's life occasioned a fuller menu at the 1977 Secret Service Christmas party. According to an internal White House memo, that menu included "cookies, fruit cake, spiced cider, and punch served in the State Dining Room, tables decorated with Christmas patchwork cloths over red felt."

The Press Preview Party and the family party for members of Congress even merited alcohol! A White House memo detailed the party plans: "Two tables with Christmas cookies, fruitcake, punch, and wine will be set up in the East Room and State Dining Room. Christmas patchwork cloths over red felt. Green garlands across." The instructions to decorate the tables with "Christmas patchwork" tablecloths and red felt with a single green garland across the front certainly are simple by today's standards. The lesson here is that Christmas decorating and entertaining do not need to be complicated or stressful. Remember Mrs. Carter when planning the holidays. A wonderful holiday celebration can be as simple as cookies, punch, and patchwork!

Rosalynn Carter's
FESTIVE BIRTHDAY-HAT ORNAMENTS

I was charmed by Mrs. Carter's inexpensive birthday-hat ornaments (my version is pictured left), which are easy to make. Mrs. Carter's ornaments paid tribute to her family peanut farm: She took a birthday party hat and replaced the elastic chin string with a lace ribbon, then filled the hat with peanuts and hung it by its lace handle on the tree. For a modern twist, you can use the ornaments as parting gifts. As guests leave, they can pick their own ornaments from your tree!

Supplies

Scissors

Birthday hats (solid colors look best)

Ribbon, 1 inch wide (a standard spool of ribbon will yield approximately two dozen "ribbon handles")

Hot-glue gun

Peanuts or a filling of your choice (see Tips)

Tips :: There are many alternatives to peanuts. For example, other types of nuts or candies, such as peppermints, gumdrops, and gum balls, will work. Paper tissue can be stuffed into the hats to reduce the amount of "filling" needed.

STEP *One* Cut the elastic band off the birthday hat.

STEP *Two* Cut the ribbon into 12-inch strips.

STEP *Three* Hot-glue the ends of the ribbon to the sides of the hat (on the inside) to create a handle.

STEP *Four* Fill with treats of your choice and hang on the tree.

6

A Hollywood Holiday

NANCY REAGAN

1981–1989

A HOLLYWOOD HOLIDAY

Nancy Reagan

"I must confess, I still believe in Santa Claus!"
—NANCY REAGAN, AS REPORTED IN THE *WASHINGTON POST*

Ever since she was a child in Chicago, Nancy Reagan loved Santa Claus and the magic of Christmas. When the Reagans moved to Washington, private Christmas traditions became public White House traditions. "I really do love Christmas," Mrs. Reagan told the *Washington Post*, "and it just seemed to come naturally to me to make it the way it's always been for me, for us."

But 1981 was not just the Reagans' first Christmas in the White House; it was also their first Christmas following the assassination attempt on the President's life the previous March. Looking back on that Christmas, what Mrs. Reagan remembered most was just how thankful she was that her husband was alive. While the official White House Christmas theme was an "Old-Fashioned Christmas with the Museum of American Folk Art," the unofficial theme of the White House was "gratitude."

The Museum of American Folk Art in New York lent Mrs. Reagan national treasures with which to decorate the White House for Christmas. The folk art celebrated both the history and the culture of America. Pieces from the museum were supplemented with newly made handicrafts, such as the seashell wreaths sprinkled with gold glitter made by fifth graders in Cape May, New Jersey. Their teacher had taught the students about this type of colonial wreath and let them craft their own in class. The teacher sent photos to the White House, and Mrs. Reagan took a liking to them. A return letter asked the students to make forty seashell wreaths for the White House Christmas decorations. There was also an authentic Victorian dollhouse on display at the Diplomatic Children's Party, complete with miniature period furniture and figures dressed in clothing made from antique fabric. Mrs. Reagan had a cherished Christmas memory of being given just such a dollhouse one Christmas. It was built especially for her by a stagehand working on a play in which her mother was acting. Mrs. Reagan shared with the *Washington Post* that "it was just wonderful. I just adored that dollhouse. It was quite large. He'd really gone to a lot of trouble."

In 1982 Mrs. Reagan had a dazzling idea for Christmas. The theme was an "Old-Fashioned Christmas with Foil Paper

PRECEDING SPREAD :: President and Mrs. Reagan's official Christmas portrait, 1987. Notice Mrs. Reagan's fancy Christmas shoes!
LEFT :: Mrs. Reagan wraps Christmas presents in the private residence in December 1982.

Cones and Snowflakes," and thousands of sparkling gold snowflakes and foil cones would adorn the official tree. To make the ornaments, the First Lady called on volunteers from Second Genesis, a residential drug-rehabilitation program. She had introduced her "Just Say No" slogan that year, as part of her drug-awareness program. Mrs. Reagan's belief in drug rehabilitation was so strong that she invited the young people from Second Genesis, many of whom had criminal records as well as dependency problems, into the most public home in the United States.

The First Lady placed her trust in the recovering drug addicts, and they repaid her by doing a wonderful job. The snowflakes and cones were made on-site at Second Genesis, and took three months to complete. When they were finally hung on the Blue Room tree, the shiny ornaments were as glitzy and glamorous as the First Lady herself. Mrs. Reagan was so impressed, Second Genesis returned for three more years as her annual elves. Dr. Sidney Shankman, the executive director of the program, wrote a touching note to Mrs. Reagan: "Our kids, once they graduate from the program, will not have easy lives. But those who worked with you last Friday will carry with them always the memory that the very gracious First Lady of the Land took time to show them her concern and her love."

The gold snowflakes joined papier-mâché angels, which were placed throughout the state rooms. And there was a second surprise ornament: In a tribute to her home state, Mrs.

LEFT :: Mrs. Reagan, hanging snowflake ornaments on the Blue Room tree, worked with volunteers from Second Genesis Drug Rehabilitation Center in 1982.

RIGHT :: Mrs. Reagan sits on Mr. T's lap and distributes gifts during the 1983 press preview of the Christmas decorations.

Reagan had over one hundred pounds of unshelled walnuts sent to the White House from California. Each walnut was wrapped in lace and hung on the Blue Room tree.

To make the ornaments, the First Lady called on volunteers from a drug-rehabilitation program.

That year Mrs. Reagan brought the magic of television to Washington, DC, with a celebrity Santa: Willard Scott, the weatherman from the *Today* show. A surprise Santa was a beloved holiday custom in the Reagan home. At the White House, Willard Scott handed out monkey bread to the press—a gift from Mrs. Reagan that would become a White House tradition during her tenure as First Lady. In the Christmas seasons that followed, Willard was followed by a series of outrageous

Hollywood Santas: *The A-Team's* Mr. T handed out Mr. T dolls to children in 1983, and in 1985, *Dallas* star Larry Hagman hung dollar bills on the White House tree. But one year, the surprise was on the First Lady—she found herself sitting on Santa's lap, only to realize it was her grown son, Ron, beneath the white beard!

In 1983 Mrs. Reagan repeated the "Old-Fashioned Christmas with Antique Toys" theme used by Mrs. Carter. Although she did not have a young child like Amy, Mrs. Reagan embraced the childlike awe of the holiday and put her own new spin on the theme. Under the tree, instead of presents or a train set, she featured an antique toy circus, while gold-foil paper chains were strung on the tree. Ever aware of the importance of the press, Mrs. Reagan posed for pictures wrapping presents and decorating both the official White House tree and the tree in the Reagans' private residence.

For Christmas 1984, volunteers from Second Genesis got a helping hand from volunteers at the Brandywine River Museum in Chadds Ford, Pennsylvania. The museum's annual Christmas display had come to the First Lady's attention. For years museum

Although she did not have a young child, Mrs. Reagan embraced the childlike awe of the holiday and put her own new spin on the theme.

volunteers crafted Christmas "critters," ornaments in the shape of enchanting woodland creatures, which were made out of natural materials like pinecones, seed pods, and dried flowers. At Mrs. Reagan's request, the museum sent over two thousand of these ornaments to

ABOVE :: An antique toy circus circled the base of the 1983 Blue Room tree. Note the Reagan's Christmas cards recycled as ornaments.

ABOVE :: Teddy Bears frolic on the wreath hanging on the landing of the Grand Staircase.

the White House, and Second Genesis volunteers hung them on the Blue Room tree. That year's theme paid homage to the ornaments and the volunteers who hung them. It was called the "Year of Second Genesis and Natural Pieces." It has also been referred to as "Enchanting Creatures."

Teddy bears, outfitted with holiday hats and scarves, made their appearance throughout the White House.

In 1985 Mrs. Reagan chose the theme of an "Old-Fashioned Christmas with Teddy Bears." Teddy bears, outfitted with holiday hats and scarves, made their appearance throughout the White House. Mrs. Reagan did not make the more conventional choice of decorating with miniature stuffed bears. She chose regular-size bears. They were placed

playfully on wreaths and ladders and on various tabletops and mantels.

That year Mrs. Reagan decided to put something dear to her heart on the official tree. The season before, the Reagans had received over forty thousand Christmas cards and well wishes from around the world. Mrs. Reagan thought it fitting to put the sentiment-filled cards on the tree. To do this, she once again turned to the ever-industrious Second Genesis volunteers. The volunteers turned their scissors to the Christmas card collection, employing a practice common in homes across America. The volunteers cut the cards and gave them ribbons, effectively recycling them into ornaments. Fifteen hundred were made in all.

When the First Lady chose "Mother Goose" as the theme in 1986, Second Genesis

RIGHT :: It's hard to spot Mrs. Reagan amongst the magnificent East Room decorations assembled for the TV taping of *Christmas Special at the White House* in December of 1986.

made hundreds of stuffed goose ornaments to illustrate the nursery rhyme. Mrs. Reagan added the artificial snow and tinsel she had so loved as a girl. This was used as a backdrop for NBC's *Christmas Special at the White House* that year. Forever cognizant of how her public image played in the press, Mrs. Reagan worked with Hollywood and New York directors to transform the East Room into a snowy wonderland, complete with Santa's sleigh in the middle of the room. There were so many trees, and so much tinsel, that it was hard to spot Mrs. Reagan when she stood in the midst of the trees and snow!

In 1987 the First Lady put a spin on Christmas that reflected one of the things she loved most about the holidays—carols. It was dubbed the year of the "Toyland Musical Tree" and has also been called a "White House

RIGHT :: President Reagan gives
Mrs. Reagan a Christmas present
in their private quarters on Christmas Eve, 1982.

FAR RIGHT :: President Reagan
decorates the family's tree in the
private residence on Christmas Eve
in 1984.

Musical Christmas." Some of Mrs. Reagan's
sweetest holiday memories centered on carols:
listening to her children sing with classmates
at school Christmas concerts, decorating the
tree with carols playing in the background,
and holding sing-alongs with family and
friends on Christmas Eve. Mrs. Reagan told
Interview magazine the story of how, when her
children became teenagers, they would always
try to replace the carols with rock and roll.
"The kids used to tease me," she said. "They'd
always try to put rock music on while we were
trimming the tree and I'd say, 'This is my day,
and we're going to have Christmas carols.'"

The "Toyland Musical Tree" was covered
with 350 wooden ornaments made by the
White House carpenters. Sheet music was
rolled up, tied with yarn, and hung as decorations from the branches. Decorations for

mantels and tabletops were inspired by popular Christmas songs, such as "Rudolph the Red-Nosed Reindeer," "Frosty the Snowman," "I Saw Mommy Kissing Santa Claus," and even "All I Want for Christmas Is My Two Front Teeth"!

In 1988, for her last Christmas in the White House, Mrs. Reagan's theme was a variation of 1985's "Old-Fashioned Christmas with Teddy Bears." In a slight change of words, 1988's theme was "Old-Fashioned Tree with Teddy Bears." The teddy bears were back, joined by new ornaments for the tree: 300 wooden candles, 100 papier-mâché hot-air balloons, 75 yarn dolls, red balls wrapped in gold mesh, and icicles made of gold beads. The White House chef echoed this playful theme when he fashioned a Christmas tree out of kale and colorful vegetables for the Reagans' Christmas dinner.

In her eight holiday seasons at the White House, Mrs. Reagan took family-friendly themes, tied them up with a shiny gold Tinseltown bow, and made certain everyone who visited the White House at Christmas was enchanted. She believed you could decorate with whatever made you happy, and fondly recalled to the *Washington Post* her first Christmas tree as a newlywed, when she decorated the tree "just with everything I could hang on it!" Mrs. Reagan loved Christmas decorating and wanted everyone to know that, "more than anything else, Christmas at the White House has always been a children's holiday."

Achoo!

In 1981 White House Christmas decorators had to revise their plans when President Reagan's allergies reacted to the live decorations and flowers. Decorators moved greens and flowers from the Yellow Oval Room, which was part of the First Family's residence, to parts of the White House infrequently visited by the President. Allergies were also a problem for President Clinton, who was known to lose his voice with prolonged exposure to fresh flowers. Both Presidents had artificial decorations in their living quarters but suffered through live Christmas trees for the sake of an amazing White House Christmas.

~ *Nancy Reagan's* ~
MONKEY BREAD

A reporter once asked Mrs. Reagan, "What's Christmas without monkey bread?" Mrs. Reagan's holiday treat was famous, and I was anxious to try it (my update on her classic rendition is pictured left). The Reagans enjoyed the sticky treat at their holiday table for years, and Mrs. Reagan later made Monkey Bread her annual gift to the White House press corps. No one was ever brave enough to ask if she thought the press was a bunch of monkeys.

Ingredients

1 (¾-ounce) package dry yeast

1 to 1¼ cup milk, at room temperature

3 eggs

3 tablespoons sugar

1 tablespoon salt

3½ cups flour

6 ounces butter, at room temperature

½ pound melted butter

Equipment

Two 9-inch ring molds

* Makes 28 rolls

Tip :: For a modern twist, try making the Monkey Bread in large muffin tins. ~

~ STEP *One* In bowl, mix yeast with part of milk [about a tablespoon] until dissolved. Add two 2 eggs [and] beat. Mix in dry ingredients. Add remaining milk a little at a time, mixing thoroughly. Cut in [room-temperature] butter until blended. Knead dough, [and] let it rise 1 to 1 and ½ hours until double in size. Knead again, let rise 40 minutes.

~ STEP *Two* Roll dough onto floured board, [and] shape into log. Cut log into 28 pieces of equal size. Shape each piece of dough into ball, [and] roll in melted butter. Use half of the pieces in each buttered, floured mold. Place 7 balls in each mold, leaving space between. Place remaining balls on top, spacing evenly. Let dough rise in mold. Brush tops with remaining egg. Bake in preheated oven at 375 [degrees] until golden brown, approximately 15 minutes.

REPRINTED WITH PERMISSION FROM
THE RONALD REAGAN PRESIDENTIAL LIBRARY

7

— *Christmas Is a Storyland* —

BARBARA BUSH

1989–1993

∼ CHRISTMAS IS A STORYLAND ∼
Barbara Bush

"We love this house, and we love sharing it—but especially now when it's so beautiful and festive at the Christmas season."

—BARBARA BUSH • 1989 • CHRISTMAS PAMPHLET

Young Barbara Pierce, age sixteen, was wearing an off-the-shoulder green-and-red dress when she met and instantly fell in love with her future husband, George "Poppy" Bush, at a Christmas dance. It was just days after the Japanese bombed Pearl Harbor in 1941. Decades later, in 1981, she became the nation's Second Lady and held that title for eight years while her husband served as Vice President under Ronald Reagan. Mrs. Bush already knew the White House well when she became First Lady upon President Bush's inauguration in 1989. The Bushes had six children—George, Robin, Jeb, Neil, Marvin, and Dorothy—and their growing family included two small grandchildren when they entered the White House. Barbara Bush was the First Lady who wanted to share the White House with everyone, and for her that started with Christmas.

Mrs. Bush's strong belief that the White House was the People's House and her joy in being a grandmother both influenced her Christmas planning, which began almost as soon as she moved in. The new First Lady was surprised to learn she needed to begin thinking about Christmas in February! The Christmas decorations had grown quite elaborate under Mrs. Reagan, and the White House florist staff and carpenters had to create many of the decorations on-site. Once she focused on the task, Mrs. Bush did not have to think long or hard about her theme—1989 would be a "Storybook Christmas."

The "Storybook Christmas" featured popular characters from children's books, and it championed a favorite cause of Mrs. Bush's: literacy. Mrs. Bush was known to wish visitors a "Merry and well-read Christmas with your own families" as they toured the decorations. The tree she placed in the Blue Room showcased eighty soft-sculpture ornaments, including Mary Poppins, the Tin Man, Pinocchio, and the Poky Little Puppy. Painted letters of the alphabet and tiny books were used as ornaments, too. Mrs. Bush also followed Nancy Reagan's example and used Mrs. Nixon's state flower balls. Gold stars and red balls filled out the tree. Beneath the tree there were books tied with ribbons. On a side table, a soft-sculpture family read "'Twas the Night Before Christmas."

In the State Dining Room, the beloved gingerbread house

PRECEDING PAGE :: For the second time in White House history, the "Nutcracker" was chosen as the official Christmas theme in 1990. Here, two large nutcracker soldiers stand guard over the Blue Room tree. RIGHT :: First Lady Barbara Bush accepts the White House Christmas tree with her granddaughter Lauren and a group of children in 1991.

ABOVE :: Bush grandchildren Sam and Ellie LeBlond play in artificial snow inside the White House, December 1991.

was displayed. Weighing in at 45 pounds, it was three feet tall and two feet wide, and it inspired the decorations for the entire dining room. The boxwood topiaries displayed on the dining table and mantel and the swags under the sconces were embellished with candy canes, lollipops, peppermints, and Christmas cookies.

That year Mrs. Bush expanded on a trend Mrs. Reagan had started. She placed multiple trees throughout the White House. In the

In the Cross Hall and Grand Foyer alone, Mrs. Bush had seventeen trees!

Cross Hall and Grand Foyer alone, Mrs. Bush had seventeen trees! These were decorated with artificial snow, tinsel, and white lights. Perhaps intending to prevent criticism over the num-

ber of trees, the White House made a point of describing the trees as "gently lit." Decorating seventeen trees with cotton bunting so they looked snow laden was a monumental task, but forty volunteers, mostly florists, gladly accepted the job. The Bushes, with extended family in tow, vacated the White House for a restaurant dinner one night so the volunteers could finish their work. Upon their return, Mrs. Bush remembered in her autobiography, her family was surprised and amused that the decorating had "disintegrated into a snowball fight," complete with cotton snowballs.

When the fake snow settled, the volunteers got back to work that night. Greenery accented with red velvet was placed throughout the state rooms. In the East Room, two fifteen-foot trees were adorned with gold and red ribbon, and the baroque Engelhard crèche, originally given to Mrs. Johnson, was displayed. Downstairs, in the East Colonnade, Mrs. Bush chose to re-create Mrs. Nixon's red poinsettia tree. The First Lady also followed another practice of Mrs. Nixon for the downstairs level. She displayed a collection of official presidential Christmas cards, starting with President Eisenhower's.

In the Yellow Oval Room, which was part of the First Family's residence, Mrs. Bush displayed a special present she'd been given. For years Mrs. Bush had done needlepoint with the women in her Episcopalian church group in Texas, who playfully called themselves the Saintly Stitchers. That fall, when the First Lady stopped at home for a visit, the stitchers gifted her with a beautiful fifty-piece needlepoint crèche—complete with some unorthodox additions. Along with the traditional Wise Men and shepherds were needlepoint replicas of Millie, the First Dog; and Bevo, the University of Texas long-horned steer mascot. Mrs. Bush absolutely loved the crèche and surprised the White House volunteer decorators that December by inviting them to the private residence to see it. It was a marvelous gift, and it inspired the First Lady's plans for a future White House Christmas.

The family Christmas tree was also in the Yellow Oval Room. It was decorated with gingerbread cookies and the family's personal ornaments. Mrs. Bush placed the tree right in front of the center window so it could be seen by visitors who came to see the National Tree on the Ellipse. With this same view in mind,

LEFT :: Two needlepoint Millie ornaments hung on the tree, including this one, made by the First Lady herself.

Mrs. Bush also had exterior wreaths with red bows hung on the three stories of windows facing the National Tree. She guaranteed that visitors to the Ellipse would have a beautiful view of the White House.

Along with the traditional Wise Men and shepherds were needlepoint replicas of Millie, the First Dog; and Bevo, the University of Texas long-horned steer mascot.

Mrs. Bush knew that her decorating impacted on the public, and that her charitable actions carried great influence, too. As she noted in her autobiography, *Barbara Bush: A Memoir,* when she heard that year most Washington, DC, shopping areas were prohibiting Salvation Army bell ringers, she exclaimed, "Who can think of Christmas without Salvation Army bell ringers?" She promptly headed to the only mall allowing the bell ringers on the property. Mrs. Bush made a very public donation of eleven dollars and effectively saved Christmas for the Salvation Army. The bell ringers were reinstated, and donations to the organization increased. Mrs. Bush so enjoyed the bell ringers, they were added to the White House entertainment during public tours, along with choirs and individual singers. Mrs. Bush fondly reminisced that her grandchildren would slip away from the family quarters and perch on the stairs to the Grand Foyer, listening to the carols and bells.

The Bushes also supported *Christmas in Washington*, which was an annual musical television program that raised funds for Children's Hospital. In 1989 Olivia Newton-John and Diahann Carroll and her husband, Vic Damone, were the guests of honor. Following the show, the President invited the singers back to the White House. George, Barbara, Olivia, and Diahann ended the night singing Christmas carols around the piano in the East Room.

The season held the usual assortment of parties, including a Press Preview Party, the Congressional Ball, and the Diplomatic Children's Party. Mrs. Bush started a new family tradition that year—the White House Christmas Family Brunch. She invited close friends and family to travel to Washington, DC, many all the way from Houston, for a holiday celebration. Later the extended Bush family packed up and headed to Camp David for the actual holiday, a custom the Bushes followed for their entire tenure in the White House.

LEFT :: Toy soldiers and ballet slippers hung on the Official Blue Room tree to celebrate the 1990 "Nutcracker" theme.

RIGHT :: The Cross Hall dazzled visitors with multiple snow-laden trees and sparkling lights.

Reflecting on the 1989 Christmas decorations, Mrs. Bush proclaimed them the most beautiful she had ever seen. But then she was known to say that every year.

The eighteen-foot Blue Room tree was decorated with oversized ornaments, including forty-five porcelain dancers and actual ballet slippers.

In 1990 Mrs. Bush chose the "Nutcracker" as her theme, in honor of the very first Christmas theme chosen by Mrs. Kennedy. The Blue Room tree was, as usual, massive—it was eighteen feet tall. That year some of the ornaments were oversized, too. Forty-five porcelain dancers, each over a foot tall, graced the official tree. In addition, the Christmas decorators were given actual ballet slippers in larger sizes to embellish. One famous ornament was a

pair of pointe shoes autographed by members of the Bolshoi Ballet. Awed by the decorations, Mrs. Bush said, "It is in the Blue Room where the magic can be most truly felt."

The 1990 Christmas season was extraordinary for a couple of reasons: Over one hundred thousand visitors came to see the Christmas decorations, providing living proof of Mrs. Bush's belief that the White House was the People's House. And the visitors were certainly amazed to see all the trees—over forty-seven of them in the White House, twinkling with fifty-four thousand lights!

President Bush enjoyed the holiday decorations and the excitement that was building in the White House, but world events still weighed on his mind. Iraq had angered many countries by invading Kuwait the previous August, and U.S. forces were in the region. It was the buildup to what soon became the Persian Gulf War. That holiday season, President Bush taped a message to be played during the Walt Disney Christmas Parade in Florida:

> This Christmas, let us pray for peace on earth, for the safe return of all of our military troops. And let us give thanks to the families who wait so patiently.

President Bush had urged Americans in his first inaugural address to be "a thousand points of light." With this phrase, he had encouraged Americans to connect with the less fortunate—through volunteerism, monetary donations, and compassion. He didn't expect that he himself would be on the receiving end of

RIGHT :: Bush grandson Sam LeBlond shows his cousin Walker the snowy town that circles the bottom of the Blue Room tree, as their moms watch nearby, 1991.

such efforts, but during the Christmas season of 1990, that's just what happened. The Bushes' home on Kennebunk Beach, Maine, had been completely destroyed by a hurricane earlier that fall, when thirty-foot waves engulfed their house. For Christmas their friends organized a gift list to replace what was lost. The list was basic—toaster, coffeemaker, can opener, lamps. Although financially sound, the Bushes nonetheless were touched by the heartfelt efforts of their friends.

For Christmas 1991, Mrs. Bush chose the theme of a "Needlepoint Christmas," inspired by the needlepoint crèche the Saintly Stitchers had given her. It was an incredible undertaking. Patterns were sent to the Saintly Stitchers and other volunteer needlepointers in March. In the end, there were over 1,370 needlepoint pieces created especially for the White House, not including the fifty-piece crèche made in 1989, which was also displayed.

White House Chief Floral Designer Nancy Clarke estimated that over 150,000 hours of labor went into making the needlepoint creations. Another 1,600 volunteer hours were needed to put the decorations in place.

According to the White House, the Blue Room was turned into a "needlepoint world of enchantment," with the bulk of the needlepoint creations used for the Blue Room tree. The needlepoint ornaments consisted of angels, gingerbread men, rocking horses, snowflakes, and candy canes. There were even two needlepoint renditions of "First Dog Millie" to put on the tree! An eighty-two-piece needlepoint village was placed under the tree, complete with an electric train to run through it. Lastly, there was a ninety-two-piece needlepoint Noah's Ark, with the animals displayed two by two.

The East Room decor changed slightly. The antique baroque Engelhard crèche resumed its normal station, flanked by two trees. Another two trees were placed on either end of the room. The mantels were covered in greens and peppered with red candles in hurricane globes. Ornaments included gold glass pinecones, strings of gold beads, and red paisley ribbon. The Grand Foyer and Cross Hall were decked with twenty-one trees in a variety of sizes, which were ornamented with Mrs. Bush's snowy signature—icicles, tinsel, and white lights.

In the State Dining Room, a garland

ABOVE :: Mrs. Bush admires the needlepoint crèche that the Saintly Stitchers church group made for her, December 1989.

encircled the large portrait of Abraham Lincoln, which now hung above the mantel. An oversized Santa was placed prominently on a center table. And the gingerbread house got a new visitor—First Dog Millie joined Hansel and Gretel.

Visitors were greeted by two eleven-foot nutcracker toy soldiers guarding snow-laden trees.

As she had in the past, Mrs. Bush worked to include Christmas decor in the downstairs South Entrance and East Colonnade. Visitors were greeted by two eleven-foot nutcracker toy soldiers guarding snow-laden trees. Wreaths hung in the windows and the poinsettia trees were again on display to dazzle visitors.

But the biggest change in 1991 was in the entertainment. The Diplomatic Children's

Party, in existence for thirty years, was no more. In its place was a children's party for local schoolchildren. Mrs. Bush said the change was in response to the many letters she had received from local schools requesting to see the White House at Christmas. Those schools that had taken the initiative to write the First Lady, such as Immaculate Conception, the Drew Model School, and the Long Branch public school, were rewarded with a coveted invitation to the East Room. The schoolchildren were treated to performances by a Russian dance troupe and a magician. But the First Lady did not forget the diplomats' children—instead of the usual party, they were given a Christmas tour while their parents had tea with Mrs. Bush. No doubt the diplomats' children missed the big East Room party, but it was probably a welcome change for their parents, who had not been invited to accompany their children in the past.

That December, there was a flurry of activity in the White House. Johnny Carson and his family came and spent the night in the Lincoln Bedroom after President Bush presented him with the Medal of Freedom award. Mrs. Bush flew to New Hampshire to file the necessary papers so her husband could seek reelection. Expectations were high for a second term thanks to the quick resolution of the Persian Gulf War the previous March. But the best gift President Bush got that year came on Christmas Day itself—Mikhail Gorbachev resigned. The Cold War was over and the Soviet Union officially was no more. The President was elated with the

thought of democracy spreading across the former Soviet Union.

The Christmas theme in 1992 was the "Gift Givers." Mrs. Bush explained that the original gift givers were the three wise men, but that gift givers had taken many forms over the ages: Santa Claus, St. Nicholas, Kris Kringle, and the Snow Maid, to name a few. That Christmas thirty trees adorned the White House, a fact that Mrs. Bush alluded to in her welcoming remarks to visitors:

⤳ I'm so pleased that all of you could be here with us today to visit your White House at Christmas, when it's at its most beautiful and fragrant, too. ⤳

The First Lady had truly achieved her goal of sharing the People's House. That year

ABOVE :: President Bush reads a Christmas story to his grandchildren at Camp David, 1991.

RIGHT :: Mrs. Bush places the star atop the National tree on the Ellipse with grandchildren Sam and Ellie in November of 1990.

120,000 visitors passed through the White House to gaze upon the Christmas decorations. The Blue Room tree was decorated with ornaments representing eighty-eight different gift givers. Tall, unlit candles and large velvet bows in red and gold were used as ornaments. In the State Dining Room, the gingerbread house was completely transformed into Santa's Village, some forty inches long and three feet high. Downstairs the eleven-foot toy nutcracker soldiers again greeted visitors as they came through the South Entrance, passing a tree hung with the needlepoint ornaments from the prior year.

Christmas 1992 was the Bushes' last in the White House. President Bush had fallen from his high public-approval ratings and had been defeated by the charismatic governor of Arkansas, Bill Clinton. The Bushes had enjoyed four fabulous White House Christmas seasons and had awakened to four Christmas mornings at Camp David. They had entered the White House with two grandchildren to spoil with Christmas cheer and left with twelve. That December Mrs. Bush spoke her final Christmas greeting as First Lady:

⌒ The President and I and all the other members of our family wish each and every one of you a Merry Christmas. ⌒

Down!
❧

Barbara Bush, the shy schoolgirl who had to muster the courage to be the angel in her school's Christmas play, had a twelve-year starring role in our nation's Christmas festivities. Starting with her first year as Second Lady, during the Reagan administration, Mrs. Bush took an often bumpy ride in a cherry picker to the very top of the National Tree on the Ellipse, which was usually about forty feet from the ground. Traditionally, the star is set in place two weeks before the President flips the lights on the tree in mid-December. Mrs. Bush had the honor of putting the star on the National Tree eight times as Second Lady and four as First Lady. Over the years, six grandchildren took the trip with her: Jenna and Barbara, Sam and Ellie, and Walker and Marshall. One year Mrs. Bush even took with her Rita and Rex, puppets from the Reading Is Fundamental literacy organization, to bring attention to her cause of promoting literacy. Each year, upon completing the vertical trip, Mrs. Bush emphatically delivered her favorite line, "Down!"

Barbara Bush's
EMBELLISHED BALLET SLIPPERS

When Mrs. Bush chose "The Nutcracker" theme, she sent artists ballet pointe shoes and asked them to embellish them. In my version (pictured left), I worked with jeweled appliques and artificial flowers. I've suggested some decoration ideas for the shoes, but this craft is wide open, so use your imagination. To complete the theme, consider using tulle as your garland. Your tree will have a magical Nutcracker effect, particularly if you are bold enough to use a white artificial tree!

Supplies

Ballet pointe shoes, preferably pale pink or cream colored

Embellishing glue for fabric (clearly labeled at craft stores)

Decorations for the shoes, such as gemstones, sequins, beads, buttons, glass, and tiles

Artificial flowers, tulle, small dolls, stuffed animals, or whatever you like to fill the shoe

STEP *One* Cover as much or as little of the shoe with decorations as you like.

STEP *Two* Tie the ribbons together so they can be hung from a branch.

STEP *Three* After the glue dries, you can also tuck items into the shoe, such as artificial flowers, tulle, small dolls, stuffed animals, or anything decorative or whimsical.

Tip :: Ballet pointe shoes, which can be purchased either new or used at dance schools or online, have a silk ribbon that can create a beautiful cascading effect when hung on a Christmas tree.

8

Winter Wonderland

HILLARY CLINTON

1993–2001

WINTER WONDERLAND

Hillary Clinton

"It's going to be a Christmas as it always is . . . just the traditional Christmas we grew up with."

—HILLARY RODHAM CLINTON, AS REPORTED IN THE *WASHINGTON POST*

It might be surprising to learn that Hillary Rodham Clinton, a successful lawyer and political activist, had a fondness for dime-store Christmas jewelry. Her holiday collection included such endearing items as a reindeer pin, a stocking pin, and a flashing green Christmas tree necklace, which she was bold enough to wear on the *Larry King Live* TV show. As First Lady, Mrs. Clinton wanted to create a traditional Christmas for her husband, President Bill Clinton, First Daughter Chelsea, and the nation. Growing up, Mrs. Clinton and her two younger brothers had enjoyed simple holidays. Christmas Eve was for baking chocolate chip cookies, making aluminum foil and pipe cleaner ornaments with their grandfather, and hanging them on the tree, whose branches always remained bare until December 24. But the contemporary needs of the White House didn't completely mesh with Mrs. Clinton's simple vision of the past. The result was a multifaceted Christmas—old-fashioned yet modern, simple but complex, much like the First Lady herself.

Mrs. Clinton still chuckles about the reminder, in June 1993, that she was behind in her Christmas planning. Like Barbara Bush before her, Mrs. Clinton had no idea that Christmas planning should start so early in the year. She quickly caught up, and chose "Angels and the Year of the American Craft" as her theme for 1993. Once it was decided, Mrs. Clinton half joked that the theme was a state secret, closely guarded until it could be revealed in December.

For "Angels and the Year of the American Craft," Mrs. Clinton reached out to one thousand artists across the country, who were instructed to make angels using their different artistic mediums. Suggestions included angels made from wood, metal, fiberglass, clay, and needlepoint. The heavenly results of the request were bountiful. Over 7,500 angel ornaments arrived from across the country in October. Most were placed on the official Blue Room tree. Mrs. Clinton joked that the Arkansas angel was smack in the front of the tree, with the angel from Al Gore's home state of Tennessee hung close by.

Captivated by the 1993 decorations, Mrs. Clinton confessed that she and the President sometimes walked the halls in the still of the night in awe of the holiday transformation.

PRECEDING SPREAD :: Chelsea hugs her father, President Clinton, in the Diplomatic Reception Room of the White House, December 18, 1995.
LEFT :: Official Christmas portrait of President and Mrs. Clinton, December 2000.

The First Lady was especially enamored with the Blue Room tree, and told the President he just might find her in a sleeping bag under its branches, as that might be the only way she could truly appreciate all the ornaments. A favorite was an angel playing the trumpet who looked a lot like the President.

Crafters also made centerpieces out of the same mediums that were used for the ornaments. The centerpieces would be used year-round and become part of the permanent White House collection. The finishing touch that Christmas was a large quilted tree skirt for the Blue Room tree. Quilters from all fifty states were asked to submit a quilted patch that best represented their state. These patches were then sewn on a beautiful green velvet skirt, which Mrs. Clinton used for each of her eight Christmases in the White House.

holiday plans so early. About 300,000 Christmas cards were sent, and 22 decorated trees, including the Blue Room tree, adorned the White House. About 2,500 musicians filled the halls with holiday harmony. And, astonishingly, 150,000 people toured the White House. To get ready for such an influx, precision was required. Perhaps the White House social secretary, Ann Stock, summed it up best in the *Washington Post*:

> It's like a battle. It takes six months to plan, and then it all has to be done in about three days.

Privately, the Clintons preserved their family Christmas traditions. Chelsea, whose name was inspired by a Christmas vacation her parents took to the Chelsea section of London, was just thirteen in 1993. That year, as the actual holiday grew closer, Chelsea and her father relished the excitement of last-minute shopping and wrapping on December 23 and 24. And although the halls of the White House had been decked since the beginning of December, the Christmas tree in the family residence was in place but undecorated. That job, in the Clintons' long-standing family tradition, wasn't even started until Christmas Eve. Stockings and family ornaments that the First Couple had collected since they were newlyweds were unpacked from boxes on the third floor. As always, the President climbed the ladder and decorated the tree (despite being allergic to it!) with his daughter. Hillary watched the scene unfold, and the three of them spent

Beyond choosing the Christmas theme, Mrs. Clinton also enjoyed planning the holiday party menus. For their first year in the White House, the Clintons hosted at least one party a day for twenty-one days straight, including parties for government officials and political supporters and the Residence Staff Party. The Clintons viewed the parties as a way to express thanks to all who helped and worked

Crafters also made centerpieces out of the same mediums used for the ornaments.

with them throughout the year. As a result, President and Mrs. Clinton stood in line, sometimes for up to four hours, greeting their guests and having photos taken.

That first year, it became clear to Mrs. Clinton why it was imperative to begin the

time remembering the history of each ornament. When the stockings were finally hung, and the fresh-baked chocolate chip cookies were eaten, the First Lady noted the White House had at last begun to feel like home.

That year Mrs. Clinton started a practice that she followed the rest of her time as First Lady.

It was, however, a Christmas tinged with sadness. President Clinton's mother, Virginia, was gravely ill with breast cancer and the President suspected it would be their last Christmas together. He convinced her to come to the White House for a week by promising to get her to Las Vegas for Barbra Streisand's New Year's Eve Concert. Virginia came and the President made good on his promise. His mother willed herself to enjoy her first and only Christmas at the White House and ring in the New Year at the concert. Sadly, she died less than a week later on January 6, 1994.

The theme for Christmas 1994 was the "Twelve Days of Christmas," and the famed designer Ralph Lauren lent his expertise to the project. Lauren's signature red-and-green tartan ribbon trimmed the greens in the Grand Foyer and Cross Hall. Subdued gold-and-burgundy ribbon was used in the East Room. Dried hydrangeas and baby's breath dipped in gold embellished the greens and trees in both locations. Artists from across America made the Blue Room tree ornaments, taking their inspiration from the song the "Twelve Days of Christmas." One humorous ornament had four birds "calling" from a phone booth.

That year Mrs. Clinton started a practice that she followed the rest of her time as First Lady. In a nod to Christmases Past, a tree that commemorated decorations from the preceding year was set up in the ground floor colonnade (the floor beneath the state rooms). In 1994 Mrs. Clinton displayed an American crafts tree with decorations from Christmas 1993.

"A Visit from Saint Nicholas" was the 1995 White House theme, which was inspired by "'Twas the Night Before Christmas," and an endearing Clinton family tradition. President Clinton had read Chelsea this poem each December since she was a baby. Once he became President, he often read the same poem to groups of schoolchildren visiting the White House. He was usually accompanied by the family cat, First Feline Socks.

LEFT :: The roping decorating the columns of the Cross Hall and Grand Foyer in 2000 was shorter than in years past and was adorned with red bows and artificial fruit.

Mrs. Clinton sought the help of three types of groups to make "A Visit from St. Nicholas" a success: architectural organizations, needlepoint guilds, and culinary schools. The ornaments from the architects and the needlepoint guild were used on the Blue Room tree. The architects' ornaments were based on the home in "'Twas the Night Before Christmas." Some were miniature houses, while others were just chimneys, roofs, windows, or porches. The needlepoint crafters sent stockings to bring to mind the phrase "the stockings were hung by the chimney with care."

The ornaments from the culinary schools hung on four large trees in the Grand Foyer and Cross Hall. Their creators had faced a special challenge: Inspired by the poem's famous phrase "and visions of sugar plums danced through their heads," the ornaments had to be entirely edible. Despite being perishable, these ornaments still had to arrive in October, and withstand time and travel. Culinary students across the country rose to the challenge, sending preserved edible ornaments made of cookie dough, marzipan, chocolate, and gingerbread.

In 1996 Mrs. Clinton revisited the "Nutcracker" theme, used previously by Jackie Kennedy and Barbara Bush.

That Christmas season a needlepoint kissing ball was introduced. Done by the master needlepoint artist Hyla Hurley, it told the story of President Clinton's journey to the White House from Hope, the evocative name of his hometown in Arkansas. Mrs. Clinton so loved the ornament, Hyla Hurley would be asked to needlepoint several more for the Clinton's White House decorations in the upcoming years.

In 1996 Mrs. Clinton revisited the "Nutcracker" theme, used previously by Jackie Kennedy and Barbara Bush. But for Mrs. Clinton, the "Nutcracker" theme was more sentimental than cultural. Chelsea had been taking dance lessons from the age of two, and the *Nutcracker* ballet held fond memories for Mrs. Clinton of watching Chelsea in recitals. Christmas 1996 was especially exciting because Chelsea had won a part in the *Nutcracker* performed by the Washington School of Ballet, where she had been studying since the family moved to the White House. Chelsea danced the role of the favorite aunt. There were a total of eighteen performances, and Chelsea shared

the role, as is customary, with another dancer. For her safety, the theater did not disclose which performances the First Daughter danced in prior to showtime.

For the "Nutcracker" theme, Mrs. Clinton once again took a three-pronged approach to tackling the Blue Room tree. That year she enlisted the help of regional and professional ballet companies, woodworking artists, and needlepointers. Of course, these artists met the White House request and created ornaments that interpreted the *Nutcracker* ballet. Mrs. Clinton was very pleased with the results and noted, "Each ornament is a charming example of the artistry and imagination found in every part of our country." The other state rooms were sprinkled with scenes from the ballet, complete with nutcrackers, fairies, ballerinas, and candies.

December 1997 found the White House celebrating the Christmas theme of "Santa's Workshop." Famous clothing designers like Oscar de la Renta, Vera Wang, and Ralph Lauren all designed fashionable Santa suits for the Blue Room tree. But the real White House news that holiday was Mrs. Clinton's choice of a Christmas present for President Clinton. After Chelsea had left for college that fall, Mrs. Clinton unexpectedly found herself experiencing the feelings of loneliness associated with an "empty nest." Her solution was to buy the President a puppy for Christmas. She picked a chocolate Lab. Suddenly the White House was bustling with puppy names. An impromptu contest ensued, with name suggestions coming from all over the country. Two of Mrs. Clinton's favorites were Clin-tin-tin and Arkanpaws. The President finally named his puppy Buddy, after his favorite uncle.

It seemed the whole country loved Buddy—except for the Clintons' cat, Socks. The two pets never got along. That Christmas season, every time the President made an appearance with schoolchildren, inevitably, their only questions concerned Buddy and Socks. The President even began posing for Christmas pictures with schoolchildren with either Buddy or Socks. That year, as children left the East Room, they were given gingerbread cookies, a box of M&Ms autographed by President Clinton, and, best of all, a picture of Socks.

Luckily the arrival of Buddy, and the ensuing drama with Socks, got the President lots of

RIGHT :: Infamous rivals, Socks and Buddy, actually pose for a picture together in the Oval Office, December 1999.

favorable press that year. That same December the Clinton administration was cast in the role of Scrooge when it decided press parties must be cut back from four parties to only two. Many questioned the wisdom of not inviting previously invited reporters, who could be venomous in print. But the reality was that the parties had grown way beyond their original purpose of thanking the reporters who actually covered the White House on a regular basis. In recent years, members of the media had descended on the parties from every part of the country, and the guest list had swelled to over two thousand journalists. During the Christmas 1997 season, the guest lists were slashed, and the White House shrewdly told the press outlets they themselves must decide who could use the limited number of invites. And it wasn't just the press parties that got an invitation overhaul. Guest lists for all White House Christmas parties were reduced by a third in an effort to limit the growing number of attendees.

When the White House cut the size of its holiday parties, it also reduced its need for sweets. Still, the White House pastry kitchen's culinary feats under the Clintons were nothing short of astounding. Even with the party cutbacks, the pastry kitchen was called on to produce 90,000 treats (as opposed to 120,000 the year before). The White House pastry chef, Roland Mesnier, first hired by Mrs. Carter, headed up the daunting sugary assignment, which proceeded with the zeal of a confectionary crusade: 250 pound cakes by July, 2,500 gingerbread cookies by August, and a total of 20,000 brownies, macaroons, pecan diamonds, hazelnut butter crescents, and linzer cookies by September. There were also 180 pumpkin, applesauce, and passion fruit cakes,

The White House pastry kitchen's culinary feats under the Clintons were nothing short of astounding.

100 coconut sheet cakes, 250 three-foot Yule logs, and thousands of truffles and miniature chocolate-and-raspberry mousses. By fall, the White House freezers were overflowing with holiday treats. An artist in the sweet kitchen, Chef Mesnier even found time to add new items as the parties approached.

In 1998 Mrs. Clinton's theme was a "Winter Wonderland." The White House's Chief Floral Designer, Nancy Clarke, teamed up with renowned New York floral designer Robert Isabell to transform the White House in a contemporary sort of way. The greatest impact was made with the twenty-four-foot exterior wreath, which weighed two thousand pounds and was hung by crane on from the Truman Balcony, on the south side of the house. Mr. Isabell made sure each light on the wreath (about 1,500 in all) was dipped in a blue gel that sparkled in the evening light. Inside the hallowed walls, a silver, gold, and crystal winter wonderland unfolded.

In the East Room, Mrs. Clinton decided on gold decor to highlight the Engelhard crèche. She took advantage of the fact that the regular chandelier was being repaired, and hung in its stead a massive Athenian wreath that was suspended from the ceiling. Ringed with electric "candles," it served as holiday replacement for the chandelier. The wreath weighed between six hundred and seven hundred pounds and was decorated with gilded leaves, white birch branches, ribbon, and tassels. Over a dozen silver and gold trees complemented the chandelier wreath and encircled the room. Large life-size angels made of natural materials heralded the birth of Christ on the mantels.

In the Grand Foyer and Cross Hall hung swags made of gold-dipped magnolia leaves, topped with silver bows and white birch branches. Modern groupings of white birch branches, lit with white lights, replaced the traditional Christmas trees of years past. In the Grand Foyer, the staircase railing was festooned with gold ribbon, white birch branches, pinecones, icicles, small hanging crystals, and white lights.

Decorations were more traditional in the Blue Room. Mrs. Clinton asked the First Lady of each state to select an artist to make a snowman (out of mediums other than snow!) that represented their state. Of course, not one state sent just one snowman. The snow people piled up, including Mrs. Clinton's favorites from Kansas—the snow Scarecrow, Tin Man, and Cowardly Lion from *The Wizard of Oz.* Also adorning the tree were hundreds of pairs of expertly knit mitten and hat ornaments. These joined handcrafted ice skates, painted sleds, and icicles. On each of the mantels in the Red and Green Rooms, the confectionary artist Colette Peters created both a delicate botanical ice castle and a snowy scene featuring igloos and penguins. Ms. Peters claimed the job was the greatest honor she'd had in her career.

In 1999 Mrs. Clinton's theme was "Holiday Treasures at the White House." In the East Colonnade, visitors were treated to the "Save America's Treasures" tree, trimmed with models of three-dimensional historic buildings that Mrs. Clinton was working to save. On the State floor for the first time anyone could remember, the Blue Room tree was lit with colored lights. It was trimmed with miniature National Historic Landmark buildings and dolls representing important Americans, such as Albert Einstein and Rosa Parks. For Mrs. Clinton the theme of "Holiday Treasures"

conjured up the feeling of an old-fashioned Christmas and, at the same time, beloved Christmas memories. She told reporters that the icicle decorations throughout the White House reminded her of snowball fights with her brothers.

The year 2000 was the Clintons' last Christmas in the White House. The theme "Holiday Reflections" was a retrospective look at each Christmas they had spent at 1600 Pennsylvania Avenue. The giant wreath from

ABOVE :: First Lady Hillary Clinton admires the Engelhard crèche in the East Room, December 1998.

RIGHT :: Socks poses next to the 1993 Gingerbread House.

During her time as First Lady, Mrs. Clinton had captured the Christmas spirit for the country.

the 1998 season was hung on the Truman Balcony. Hyla Hurley sent her last needlepoint kissing ball to Mrs. Clinton, which was hung in the Grand Foyer. The foyer columns were adorned with breathtaking roping, which was ornamented with fruit and punctuated with beautiful red bows. The best and brightest of all the Clinton ornaments were displayed on the Blue Room tree.

During her time as First Lady, Mrs. Clinton had captured the Christmas spirit for the country. The little girl who had once fainted from the heat when playing the angel in the school Christmas play found her breath and took our country to dizzying Christmas heights. And through it all, she made it clear that it was the simple things that counted most—helping others, being with family, and taking the time to enjoy small pleasures like a chocolate chip Christmas cookie. These core values guided Mrs. Clinton when she became the only First Lady to be elected a U.S. senator, to run for President, and to serve as secretary of state.

THE *Gingerbread* HOUSE

Gingerbread houses became an annual Christmas tradition in the White House during Mrs. Nixon's tenure as First Lady. That year the White House assistant pastry chef Hans Raffert created a "Hansel and Gretel" gingerbread house that weighed twenty pounds. For years the gingerbread house went unchanged, except for tiny details like a jelly bean path that celebrated President Reagan's love for the candies.

In 1992 Roland Mesnier, first hired by Mrs. Carter, took over as White House pastry chef. In 2000, he built a gingerbread village, in addition to the traditional gingerbread White House. That year Chef Mesnier replaced Santa's sled with a big red apple, to recognize that Mrs. Clinton had just been elected the next U.S. senator from the state of New York.

Chef Mesnier retired during Mrs. Laura Bush's tenure. Current White House pastry chef, Bill Yosses, put his own signature on the gingerbread house. For four seasons, starting in 2007, he replicated the White House in smooth white chocolate, with a concealed gingerbread infrastructure. It weighed three hundred and fifty pounds, and included an electric hanging light.

In 2009, at Mrs. Obama's request, Chef Yosses gave the ingredients in the gingerbread house a healthy overhaul and replaced the white sugar with honey produced in the White House's beehives. He also added Mrs. Obama's vegetable garden and a window through which to look inside the State Dining Room, where visitors could see a shining chandelier. In 2010, the gingerbread house tipped the scales at four hundred pounds, and included a giant replica of First Dog, Bo, in front of the house.

Hillary Clinton's
CHOCOLATE CHIP COOKIES

I was thrilled to bake Hillary Clinton's famous chocolate chip cookies (pictured left). Mrs. Clinton has wonderful Christmas memories of baking chocolate chip cookies with her family, first as a young girl and later with her daughter, Chelsea. During the 1992 election, Mrs. Clinton used her recipe in a bake-off against Barbara Bush, and she won! She took her recipe all the way to the White House. Enjoy these cookies at Christmas with warm milk, hot cocoa, or eggnog.

Ingredients

1½ cups unsifted all-purpose flour

1 teaspoon salt

1 teaspoon baking soda

1 cup solid vegetable shortening

1 cup firmly packed light brown sugar

½ cup granulated sugar

1 teaspoon vanilla [extract]

2 eggs

2 cups old-fashioned rolled oats

1 (12-ounce) package semi-sweet chocolate chips

* Makes 5 dozen

STEP *One* Preheat oven to 350 degrees. Grease baking sheets.

STEP *Two* Combine flour, salt, and baking soda.

STEP *Three* Beat together shortening, sugars, and vanilla in a large bowl until creamy. Add eggs, beating until light and fluffy. Gradually beat in flour mixture and rolled oats. Stir in chocolate chips.

STEP *Four* Drop batter by well-rounded teaspoonful onto greased baking sheets. Bake 8 to 10 minute or until golden. Cool cookies on sheets on wire rack for 2 minutes. Remove cookies to wire rack to cool completely.

REPRINTED WITH PERMISSION FROM
THE WILLIAM J. CLINTON PRESIDENTIAL LIBRARY

Tip :: Homemade cookies make a wonderful Christmas present. Present your cookies in a gift bag, cookie jar, or on a plate to give them a festive touch.

9

Red, White, and Blue Christmas ——

LAURA BUSH

2001 – 2009

⟲ RED, WHITE, AND BLUE CHRISTMAS ⟳

Laura Bush

"That season the White House had the quality of stillness after a snow. Almost no one was allowed in to see the decorations."

—LAURA BUSH, REFLECTING ON CHRISTMAS 2001 • FROM *SPOKEN FROM THE HEART*

No one was prepared for the 9/11 attacks and their aftermath, including President George W. Bush and First Lady Laura Bush, who had moved into the White House just nine months earlier. The terrorist attacks touched every aspect of American life in 2001, and even impacted on the Christmas decorations at 1600 Pennsylvania Avenue.

Mrs. Bush had chosen her theme "Home for the Holidays" the previous summer, when her daughters, First Twins Barbara and Jenna, were preparing to start their sophomore year in college. Perhaps Mrs. Bush was thinking ahead to when her daughters would be home for Christmas break, or maybe she simply found holiday comfort in home and family. Regardless, her theme took on greater significance once America was at war.

Sadly, the White House was officially closed for Christmas because of security concerns. There would be no tours, candlelight or otherwise. With the country on high alert, Christmas parties were also canceled. Few guests were invited to the White House that December, and some of those who were invited declined to come because they feared the White House would be a terrorist target.

Despite the lack of visitors in 2001, the White House Christmas decorators carried out the plans Mrs. Bush had created the previous summer. "Home for the Holidays" was a white Christmas, with splashes of silver, gold, and crystal. Artists from around the country contributed white ornaments depicting significant homes and places of worship from their states. These hung on the Blue Room tree. Obvious choices, like the Biltmore mansion in North Carolina, joined simple homesteads hanging on the official tree. The white ornaments were crafted from a variety of textiles, including quilted fabrics and paper. The artists called attention to detail by using shades of white: pure white, pearl white, off-white, and grayish white.

The White House residence staff were offered the opportunity to craft miniature replicas of the homes of American Presidents. White House carpenters, electricians, and plumbers happily participated. The result was eighteen well-crafted and highly detailed model homes, including Thomas Jefferson's

PRECEDING SPREAD :: In 2006, the East Colonnade was decorated with beautiful wreaths and large ornament topiaries like these in drums.
LEFT :: First Lady Laura Bush walks from the Cross Hall into the East Room to reveal the 2008 Christmas decorations to the press.

ABOVE :: The 2001 theme "Home for the Holidays," featured miniature replicas of Presidential homes. This is President Buchanan's home in Lancaster, Pennsylvania.

RIGHT :: The Grand Foyer glows with Christmas lights, as a marine pianist fills the air with Christmas music, December 2004.

Floral Designer, Nancy Clarke, demonstrated for the decorators the proper technique for applying snow: She simply picked up the snow and threw it on the tree. What happened next was to be expected. A mini-snowball fight broke out, harkening back to a similar one during the tenure of Barbara Bush, the new First Lady's mother-in-law!

In the State Dining Room, green roping was trimmed with wide white ribbon, snowflakes, and lights. In what eventually became a signature of Mrs. Bush's style, the roping went all the way to the floor and pooled in a circle. On the long dining room table were figures of Christmas carolers, standing several feet tall and dressed in white. Down the hall, in the Green Room, a beautiful silver topiary was created using silver ornaments and a champagne bucket.

Mrs. Bush achieved her goal of creating a magical Christmas experience. As she had intended, all the lights and glitter were reflected on the marble floors and the walls. The challenge now was how to share this experience with the public, since no tours were allowed. The White House Visitor Center offered one solution to the problem. Samples of the Christmas decor were displayed there, accompanied by a ten-minute video featuring Mrs. Bush and the decorations. Mrs. Bush also participated, as had Mrs. Clinton before her, in a TV program produced by HGTV called *White House Christmas,* which showcased the holiday finery. The White House website also posted a 360-degree virtual tour of the decorations.

Monticello, George Washington's Mount Vernon, and Woodrow Wilson's house, to name a few. All were given tiny wreaths with red bows and were dusted with snow. The model homes were located on tables and mantels throughout the state floor and ground floor.

Forty-nine trees shimmered throughout the house, most trimmed with white lights, tinsel, snowflakes, icicles, and gold pinecones. The finishing touch on each tree was the application of eight hundred pounds of loose artificial snow, which weighed down the tree

As Mrs. Bush had intended, all the lights and glitter were reflected on the marble floors and the walls.

branches and created drifts on the floor beneath the trees. The snow was applied in an untraditional fashion. The White House Chief

That year the Bush family spent Christmas Day at Camp David, a tradition they often repeated. President Bush took time to call nine different servicemen and servicewomen from Camp David to express his gratitude.

Mrs. Bush chose "All Creatures Great and Small" for the 2002 theme, though the White House doors remained shuttered to the public. Red and gold dominated the color scheme, and the green garlands were covered with assorted artificial fruit. As Mrs. Bush described her vision of "All Creatures Great and Small" to the press, First Dogs Barney and Spotty, a Scottish terrier and an English springer spaniel, respectively, scampered across the marble floors as if on cue. That year papier-mâché replicas of twenty-five First Pets were made and displayed under the portraits of their presidential owners. Notably missing were President Clinton's pets, Socks and Buddy, because President Clinton's portrait had not yet been completed.

Barney and Spotty played starring roles in the Bushes' new idea for bringing the 2002 Christmas decor to the people: "the Barney Cam." The Barney Cam followed Barney and Spotty as they frolicked through the White

That year papier-mâché replicas of twenty-five First Pets were made and displayed under the portraits of their presidential owners.

House, discovering the Christmas decorations. Barney actually wore a small camera, and the footage was posted on the official White House website. During the Christmas seasons that followed, the story line for Barney and pals became more elaborate, and even the

ABOVE :: Festive red-bowed wreaths hung in each window of the East Colonnade in 2006. Red ornament topiaries stood close by.

Bushes' reluctant cat, India, joined the fun. The videos evolved into mini-movies with scripts and cameo appearances by White House staffers and even the President himself. The movies were fun to watch, and also to make—one White House staffer became expert at his annual video job. Each year, he threw a large basket of ornaments in the East Room for Barney to wildly chase.

In 2003, with the White House still closed to visitors, Mrs. Bush chose a "Season of Stories" as her theme. She wished Americans "happy reading adventures and joyful holidays to all" on the White House website. A former second-grade schoolteacher and librarian, Mrs. Bush loved books, and she had even established a national semiannual book festival. Choosing a "Season of Stories" allowed her to advance a cause she loved, literacy, and pay homage to her mother-in-law, Barbara Bush, who used the "Storybook Christmas" theme in 1989. Laura Bush explained that it was great fun to be able to use some of her mother-in-law's ornaments, just as it is in many families when ornaments are passed down from one generation to the next and are lovingly reused each year.

Out came the cherished 1989 soft sculpture ornaments of literary figures. These were featured on the Blue Room tree, and beneath its branches, books of every shape and size were displayed as presents. New for the "Season of Stories" decor were intricate three-foot dolls representing characters from children's literature. The White House flower shop made

LEFT :: The White House Flower Shop created lifelike dolls from Lewis Caroll's *Alice's Adventures in Wonderland* in 2003. They were displayed on the main table in the State Dining Room.

these with inexpensive dolls, which they transformed by sewing them new costumes and painting their faces. Mrs. Bush chose the characters from stories her daughters loved as chil-

Soft sculpture ornaments of literary figures were featured in the Blue Room tree.

dren, books her students enjoyed, and favorites from her own reading adventures. Frog and Toad, the Cat from *The Cat in the Hat*, Nancy Drew, and even Harry Potter were scattered throughout the state rooms. Prominently placed on the State Dining Room table was an elaborate tribute to *Alice in Wonderland*, complete with Alice, the Rabbit, the Queen of Hearts, Tweedledee, and Tweedledum.

The coordinating element of a "Season of Stories" was candy. All of the garlands were

made with artificial candy, including large candy canes, lollipops, gumdrops, and peppermints. The four trees in the East Room were smothered in the candy-themed decorations. Smack in the center of the room, the masterful White House executive pastry chef, Roland Mesnier, made a magical Willy Wonka's chocolate factory out of chocolate. There were chocolate bolts, ladders, slides, and downspouts, which spilled chocolate onto cakes below, amazing everyone who saw it. In addition to the chocolate factory, Chef Mesnier still had time to make the traditional gingerbread house.

That December Mrs. Bush found herself behind in her Christmas shopping, even though her twins had emailed their Christmas lists early in the season. Still, Mrs. Bush and the President made time to have an East Room

party for the children of military personnel serving overseas. The children were amazed by four enormous twelve-foot nutcrackers, inspired by the ones once used by Barbara Bush, which greeted them in the Grand Foyer. They were then treated to a performance of the *Nutcracker* ballet. This event was a public display of Mrs. Bush's heartfelt message to the nation that holiday season to give support and love to military families.

In the center of the East Room, executive pastry chef, Roland Mesnier, made a magical Willy Wonka's chocolate factory out of chocolate.

Christmas 2004 was a "Season of Merriment and Melody," and it marked the joyful return of the White House Christmas tours. Doors were opened to the public, but the process was more cumbersome than just waiting in line for tickets. Now interested citizens had to write their congressperson months in advance to get the treasured admission. Forty-four thousand people toured the White House that year, which was significantly less than the 150,000 high of the Clinton administration. Christmas visitors were treated to icicle trees and musical vignettes that conjured up Mrs. Reagan's 1987 "Toyland Musical Tree" theme. Tabletop displays illustrating "Frosty the Snowman" and "I Saw Mommy Kissing Santa Claus" certainly brought smiles to the tourists.

December 2004 ended on a tragic note when a tsunami hit Southeast Asia and the coast of Africa. President Bush immediately reached out to his father, former president George H. W. Bush, and former president Bill

Mrs. Bush liked topiaries made with ornaments, and she decided to use more of them that season.

Clinton to spearhead charitable relief efforts. Then in August 2005, Hurricane Katrina struck New Orleans and the Gulf Coast, with devastating effects. Both events influenced Mrs. Bush's theme for Christmas 2005, which was "All Things Bright and Beautiful."

By choosing "All Things Bright and Beautiful," Mrs. Bush highlighted the beauty and goodness of nature in a year when its powerful forces caused heartbreaking destruction. The First Lady wanted to remind Americans that nature was also a blessing. That Christmas season the garlands were strung with what one might find in a garden, mostly an abundance of fruits and flowers. The official Christmas card featured the White House cloaked in a blanket of snow with First Dogs Barney and Miss Beazley (a second Scottish terrier, new to the Bush family that year) conveying holiday cheer.

In 2006 Mrs. Bush chose the theme "Deck the Halls and Welcome All." Green reindeer topiaries greeted guests as they entered through the East Colonnade, passing by the now annual red poinsettia trees. Upstairs the color scheme included shades of red, such as scarlet, crimson, and fuchsia. The Blue Room tree was simple, yet elegant. It was strung with beads, and iridescent glass ornaments swung from the branches. Mrs. Bush liked topiaries made with ornaments, and she decided to use more of them that season. Multiple round topiaries were created using red glass ornaments in different sizes. In the State Dining Room, tabletop topiaries, about two feet tall, were secured in red painted wooden drums that recalled colonial times. To complement the smaller topiaries, oversized, free-standing topiaries made from red ornaments were placed in the Colonnade. A tall tree made from red ornaments completed the decorating plan on the lower floor.

Concern for America's active troops and newly disabled veterans guided the Bushes' activities that December once again. Together they toured Walter Reed Army Medical Center, thanking injured veterans. Then they took part in a gift-wrapping activity with a group of school-age children from veterans' families. Gifts were donated, wrapped, and later given to families who had temporarily relocated to the DC area to be with their war-injured loved ones, still hospitalized that Christmas. Later, in what had become a more recent tradition, the First Couple hosted a military children's party where the President told the children:

> ◌ I know it's tough to have your mom or dad overseas, and we wish you all the best. But it's really important work. And so we wanted to welcome you here to the White House to, first of all, thank you for your strength, and so that you would do me a favor and email your mom or dad who is overseas how much the Commander in Chief respects them, admires them, and supports them. ◌

In 2007 Mrs. Bush chose a theme that again drew attention to nature. She called it "Holiday in the National Parks." The First Lady was an ardent lover of the outdoors. Many years before, she had resolved, with a group of women friends, to celebrate their fortieth birthdays by going hiking in many of America's natural wonders, like the Grand Canyon and Yellowstone National Park. Reflecting back on these experiences, the First Lady decided to share her love and appreciation of our national parks with the public. She also wanted people to know that our national park system includes historic sites

Mrs. Laura Bush
requests the pleasure of your company
at a Holiday Open House to be held at
The White House
on Tuesday, December 2, 2008
at two o'clock

East Entrance

and monuments like Gettysburg and the Statue of Liberty.

There are a total of 391 national parks and historic sites. Mrs. Bush sent the staff at each one a gold ball and asked them to create a representative ornament, which would be placed on the Blue Room tree. Among the ornaments were those paying tribute to the San Antonio Missions, Mount Rushmore, and the site in Pennsylvania of the crash of Flight 93 during the 9/11 attacks. On a lighter note, the pastry kitchen baked thousands of cookies representing Barney and Miss Beazley, both of whom truly loved to romp outdoors.

The 2008 season was Mrs. Bush's last Christmas as First Lady. The previous May, her family had grown by one when daughter Jenna married her longtime boyfriend, Henry Hager, at the Bush ranch. Always interested in her

ABOVE :: Author's invitation from First Lady Laura Bush to attend the unveiling of the 2008 White House Christmas decorations.

RIGHT :: President and Mrs. Bush enjoy a dance at the Congressional Ball.

correspondence from the American people, Mrs. Bush noted that many letters were requesting a patriotic Christmas for the last year of her husband's administration. Mrs. Bush gave the people what they wanted: 2008 was a "Red, White, and Blue Christmas."

Giant nutcrackers, inspired by the ones First Lady Barbara Bush used, were dressed in red, white, and blue and fashioned like Uncle Sam.

The "Red, White, and Blue Christmas" was fitting because it was an election year, with an inauguration coming soon after Christmas. The giant nutcrackers in the White House collection were given a red, white, and blue wardrobe change and made to look like Uncle Sam. Two were stationed at the East Wing entrance to the White House. Taking the

theme further, a red, white, and blue St. Nick welcomed visitors just inside the East Entrance doors. He was riding the large sleigh once used by Mrs. Reagan in the East Room. The colonnade windows each got a wreath, and in a new twist, the poinsettia tree was assembled with 250 red, white, and pink poinsettias. On the ground floor, Mrs. Bush displayed six of the nineteen miniature presidential homes from "Home for the Holidays," the theme for 2001. By reusing her decorations, Mrs. Bush explained she was just like millions of Americans who rummaged around in their attics until they found cherished old objects.

That year volunteer decorators, fingers going numb, made over three hundred large red moiré bows, which were attached to wreaths and roping both inside and outside the White House. Traditional ball-shaped green topiary plants were planted in hand-painted light blue drums, painstakingly detailed with motifs from the Federal Period, such as eagles and flags. These sat on the State Dining Room table. The roping around the fireplace and around Abraham Lincoln's portrait was decorated with large red and silver ornaments and reproductions of the Old Guard Fife and Drum Corps' iconic image of the three Revolutionary soldiers. Miniature Revolutionary drums were placed on the green swags hanging from the wall sconces. The gingerbread house, a replica of the White House, was done entirely in white chocolate, and weighed 475 pounds. Small Barney and Miss Beazley figurines rode in Santa's sleigh.

In the Blue Room, members of congress selected artists to make glass ornaments that best represented their districts. In the end, a total of 369 balls were sent. The tree was then designed on a grid, and each ornament was assigned an exact coordinate. This was done so the ornaments could be quickly found if any of the artists visited the tree. Below the tree, a moss tree skirt swept the floor. It was made by volunteers, who applied florist moss to burlap. The patriotic theme carried into the Red and Green Rooms. In the Red Room, the traditional cranberry tree was displayed for the thirty-third year. Silver eagles dotted the roping in the Green Room, and the champagne bucket topiary, crafted from silver ornaments, returned for another holiday season.

Twenty-seven trees were decorated in 2008. The fourteen in the Grand Foyer and

Cross Hall were snow laden, but without tinsel. The trees were supposed to look as they would in a forest after a snowfall. Swags and roping were adorned with red, white, and blue silk scarves, used as garland.

In the East Room, the Engelhard crèche was displayed along with two fifteen-foot trees, decorated in red, white, and blue balls. The roping on the mantels and over the large mirrors reflected the style of the trees. When it looked like the decorators might not finish by their deadline, President Bush, accompanied by an entourage from the Secret Service, made a surprise visit and gave them a pep talk in the Grand Lobby. He thanked everyone for their hard work, and joked they should come decorate his Texas ranch the next year. Inspired by the President, the tired volunteers finished the enormous decorating job on time.

ABOVE :: Mrs. Bush presents pastry chef Mesnier's 2006 gingerbread house—complete with hundreds of snowflakes!

RIGHT :: In 2001, for the first time in history a Hanukkah menorah was lit in the White House private residence.

That Christmas 700 gallons of eggnog were sipped, and 22,000 cookies—mostly Barneys and Miss Beazleys—were nibbled. Another 250 coconut cakes were consumed. This cake was Mrs. Bush's favorite from her childhood and brought back warm childhood memories. She used to get a coconut in her Christmas stocking, and her father would crack it. Then her grandmother used it to bake coconut cake. Mrs. Bush couldn't give the White House the recipe because her grandmother baked it from memory. One thing she did remember: The freshly shredded coconut scattered atop the sweet dessert looked like freshly fallen snow. The White House pastry chefs made sure to copy that detail.

George W. and Laura Bush and their daughters, Jenna and Barbara, had awakened at Camp David on twelve Christmas mornings, a record not soon to be broken. Four were during George H.W. Bush's presidency, and the last eight when the younger George Bush was President. Now, as the First Lady prepared to move back to Texas with her "windshield cowboy" (so named because GWB drove a pickup on the ranch), she joked that the next year they would be decorating their own tree—if they remembered how!

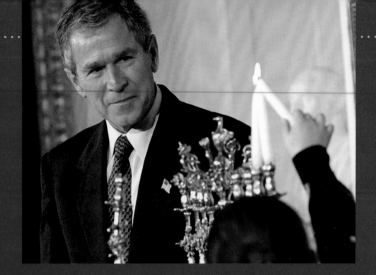

World Religions at the
White House

Contemporary U.S. presidents have made an effort to acknowledge and welcome the traditions of other world religions, in addition to Christianity. In 2001 President George W. Bush was the first President to light a menorah, or Hanukkah candelabra, in the private residence. He continued this tradition throughout his presidency. In 2007 President Bush was honored when Ruth and Judea Pearl, the parents of the slain journalist Daniel Pearl, brought their family menorah, belonging to Daniel's great-grandfather, to the White House and shared it with the nation by lighting it in the Grand Lobby. President Bush's popular press secretary, Ari Fleischer, who is Jewish, applauded the President's commitment to Judaism. Additionally, Presidents Carter, Reagan, Bush Sr., Clinton, and Obama all participated in Hanukkah ceremonies.

President and Mrs. Clinton were strongly committed to world religions. The Clintons were the first to light a menorah in the Oval Office. President and Mrs. Clinton also honored Ramadan and Kwanzaa. Mrs. Clinton felt that acknowledgment of and respect for diverse religious beliefs were essential for attaining world peace.

In 2010 President Obama hosted a Hanukkah party on the State Floor for five hundred guests. The menorah, recovered from the debris of Hurricane Katrina, was on loan from Congregation Beth Israel in New Orleans. The menorah was lit by Susan and Molly Retik, who lost their husband and father, David Retik, in the 9/11 terrorist attacks.

Laura Bush's
SHIMMERING TOPIARY CHAMPAGNE BUCKETS

I knew when I made Mrs. Bush's stunning ornament topiary (pictured left), it would delight all who saw it. Placed in a silver champagne bucket, this amazing decoration is all you need for a show-stopping table centerpiece, either in an entranceway or a dining room.

STEP One Wrap the dowel with your ribbon of choice.

STEP Two Spray-paint the Styrofoam ball the color of your ornaments to camouflage any Styrofoam that may peek through. Let dry.

STEP Three Cut the Styrofoam block so it will fit tightly in the bottom of the bucket. Cut a hole in the center of the Styrofoam block for the dowel to snugly fit, and put the Styrofoam block in the bucket. Put the dowel through the hole. If needed, insert more Styrofoam into the bucket so the dowel is secure. Use the low-heat glue to secure everything in place.

STEP Four Cut a hole in the bottom of the Styrofoam ball. Insert the dowel into the hole, and affix with low-heat glue. The basic shape of your topiary is in place.

STEP Five Over low heat, melt enough of the glue sticks in an electric frying pan or slow cooker to cover the bottom of the pan. Using the biggest ornaments first, begin to cover the Styrofoam ball by dipping each ornament top or clasp into the glue and affixing it to the topiary ball. (The ornament top or clasp must face down when glued. Ultimately, you will see only the bottoms of the balls.) Fill in the spaces with medium and small balls, until the entire surface is covered. If you are having difficulty covering space between ornaments, simply insert same colored floral picks.

STEP Six Fill in the area surrounding the dowel at the top of the ice bucket with glass beads, floral moss, or artificial ivy.

Tips: You can find the Styrofoam block and ball at craft stores, and dowels at hardware or home-improvement stores.

Supplies » 1 wooden dowel, 18 inches long (cut to size at store) » Ribbon, at least 3 inches wide » Spray paint (the color of your ornaments) » Styrofoam ball approximately the same diameter as the width of the ice bucket » Sharp knife to cut Styrofoam » Styrofoam block » Low-heat glue gun, plus extra hot-glue sticks » 1 silver-plated champagne or ice bucket » Electric frying pan or slow cooker » Plastic ornaments in a single color, in 3 sizes—small, medium, large » Glass beads, floral moss, artificial ivy, or floral picks

10

Simple Gifts —

MICHELLE OBAMA

2009–

SIMPLE GIFTS

Michelle Obama

"Because in the end, the greatest blessings of them all are the ones that don't cost a thing."

—MICHELLE OBAMA, REMARKS MADE AT THE PRESS PREVIEW,

CHRISTMAS 2010

Barack Obama, a freshman Senator from Illinois, rose on a remarkable political trajectory that brought him, and his wife, Michelle, to the White House in 2009. With them came their daughters—Malia, age eleven, and Sasha, age nine—and "grandmother-in-chief" Marian Robinson, the President's mother-in-law. Just four years before, home was a condominium in Chicago's East Park View community. Now they welcomed Christmas in their newest home, the White House. Christmas at the White House was one of Mrs. Obama's favorite experiences that year. And since she had never visited 1600 Pennsylvania Avenue during the holidays, it was completely new to her. She wanted to share the White House Christmas magic with as many people as possible. Like Barbara Bush before her, Mrs. Obama believed the White House was the People's House, and planned Christmas accordingly.

For Christmas 2009, Mrs. Obama chose the theme "Reflect, Rejoice, Renew." She explained the theme was actually a long-standing tradition for her and the President:

And for the Obama family, Christmas and the New Year has always been a time to reflect on our many blessings, to rejoice in the pleasure of spending time with our family and friends, and to renew our commitment to one another and the causes we believe in.

Over the years, their commitment to reflect, rejoice, and renew brought the Obama family strength and joy. Now Mrs. Obama chose her own family's theme as the holiday theme for the country, and she hoped it would reap the same positive benefits that her own family did.

There were important considerations that Mrs. Obama took into account for the holiday planning. A proponent of healthy eating, the First Lady took great pride and pleasure in the White House garden, which her family had planted with the help of schoolchildren from a local elementary school. Mrs. Obama wanted to find a way to bring the goodness of the garden into the holiday decorations. Second, she wished to find innovative ways to reuse existing ornaments. She turned to

PRECEDING PAGE :: President Barack Obama and First Lady Michelle Obama descend the Grand Staircase to attend a Christmas party, 2009.
RIGHT :: The 2010 Official White House Blue Room Christmas tree.

Simon Doonan, the creative director of the Barneys department store in New York City, to execute her 2009 Christmas vision.

Mr. Doonan began with a trip to the White House warehouse, in an undisclosed location in Maryland, where seasonal items

Mrs. Obama wanted to find a way to bring the goodness of the garden into the holiday decorations.

like holiday decorations are stored. Sorting through the Christmas decorations, Mr. Doonan identified hundreds of large plastic balls that could be recycled to fit the theme for 2009. These would be used for the official Blue Room tree.

The original plan was to have the balls painted by young children from all over the United States. The First Lady revised this idea,

preferring that the plastic balls be decorated by artists of all ages, with each one illustrating an important place or historic monument. And instead of painting the balls, the artists were asked to decoupage the ornaments with pictures representing their subject. When they shipped the plastic ornaments, the White House staff even included a jar of Mod Podge, a clear glue that is painted directly over the picture, to make sure the job got done.

Sixty community groups across the country were each sent ten of the recycled ornaments. One group consisted of students from the Chancellor Avenue School, an elementary school in Newark, New Jersey. Once named the most dangerous city in America, Newark was fighting to turn itself around, and the students at Chancellor were working hard in school to do their part. Recommended by a member of President Obama's urban-policy working group, the Chancellor Avenue School was elated at the opportunity to help the Obamas celebrate Christmas. Ten students were rewarded for their academic and artistic commitment, and each was given a ball to decoupage. They made ornaments representing the state capitol in Trenton, the New York Giants new stadium in the Meadowlands, and their own school building.

The Chancellor Avenue School ornaments joined others representing national treasures like the Kennedy Space Center, Mount Rushmore, and even Davy Crockett's birthplace on the evergreen branches of the Blue Room tree. There were six hundred recycled ornaments altogether. The ornaments were strung on blue ribbon, on which Girl Scout troops had hand embroidered the words "reflect, rejoice, renew" in several languages. Wide gold ribbon encircled the tree, culminating with a big bow as a tree topper.

Elsewhere in the White House, dried hydrangea sprigs were used to decorate trees and greens, repeating a floral preference first used by Ralph Lauren for Mrs. Clinton in 1994 for the "Twelve Days of Christmas." This time, however, most of the 550 dried hydrangea sprigs were dried from live floral arrangements previously used in the White House. The hydrangeas joined pepper berries, pine garlands, pinecones, and dried fruits and root vegetables from Mrs. Obama's garden as decorations throughout the house.

Four East Room trees, done in artificial

beaded fruit and dried blue hydrangeas, coordinated with four five-foot wreaths in the East Room windows. The four fireplaces were decked with garlands, and roping surrounded the mirrors above. The Engelhard crèche was displayed in its traditional niche. In the Green Room, two trees were trimmed with dried California red peppers. And in the Red Room, the cranberry tree was retired after thirty-three

Students made ornaments representing the state capitol in Trenton, the New York Giants new stadium in the Meadowlands, and their own school building.

years as a decorating staple. It was replaced by a thick, lush cranberry vine that covered the mantel, while each of the two carved marble figurines on the fireplace wore a cranberry-wreath necklace.

ABOVE :: A cranberry garland replaced the traditional cranberry tree in the Red Room in 2009. The figurines on either side of the marble fireplace were each given a cranberry necklace.

In the State Dining Room, two trees edged the sides of Abraham Lincoln's portrait. Bunches of dried burgundy hydrangeas, berries, pinecones, and gold balls complemented the deep-burgundy ribbons that cascaded down the sides of the trees. Nearby the white chocolate gingerbread house was once again an exact replica of the White House, but this time it paid tribute to Mrs. Obama's garden. It weighed in at 390 pounds, 30 of which was honey from the White House beehives. Rows of "fresh" marzipan vegetables grew in the gingerbread garden, and an edible version of First Dog Bo, given to Sasha and Malia by the late senator Ted Kennedy, played on the lawn. Visitors peeked into the State Dining Room through a window, and saw an electrified dollhouse chandelier casting light on furniture made of dark chocolate.

One last tree graced the White House. Located on the ground level, it was made entirely of cut cardboard and had thousands of tiny slots in it. It was called the Wishing Tree, and guests were invited to use colorful paper to write down their wishes, roll them up, and place them in the tree. With the recent deployment of thirty thousand additional troops to Iraq, many that year wished for world peace. For his part, President Obama wished for the American people to have confidence as they faced their future, which he believed to be extremely bright despite the ailing economy.

Keeping all the White House trees straight was no easy task, as the Obamas themselves

demonstrated when the First Lady, Malia, and Sasha visited the Children's National Medical Center in Washington, DC. After Malia and Sasha took turns reading Christmas stories to the children, the audience wondered how many trees actually adorned the White House, and the Obamas laughingly tried to recall (see facing page).

That year there were twenty-seven White House Christmas trees! In addition to keeping the trees straight, the new First Family had some other pressing holiday issues to figure out. With twenty-eight chimneys in the White House, which one would Santa use? It was determined the fireplace in the Yellow Oval Room was the most likely candidate, and the Obama family placed their tree near it. And what to leave Santa as a snack? Mrs. Obama had made an effort to leave bowls

ABOVE :: In 2009, the gingerbread house was covered in white chocolate. A perfect replica of the White House, it even featured Mrs. Obama's garden.

RIGHT :: Because the Blue Room tree towers over twenty feet, Christmas decorators have to make use of scaffolding to get the job done.

CHRISTMAS

When the First Lady and her daughters, Malia and Sasha, were asked during a 2010 visit to the Children's National Medical Center how many Christmas trees adorned the White House, their answers revealed the sheer scale of decorating for the holidays.

Q:
How many Christmas trees are in the
White House?

MRS. OBAMA:
How many Christmas trees are in the
White House? How many total are there?
There are a lot.

MALIA:
Like, okay, well, let's see, one, two, three . . .

MRS. OBAMA:
No, wait. (Laughter.) I think it's twenty-four.
I think—where's my team? (Laughter.) It's
like twenty-four . . . or twenty-six.

SASHA:
Twenty-six.

MRS. OBAMA:
Twenty-six. See, I knew I was close.
Yes, that's a lot of Christmas.

MALIA:
Unfortunately, you don't get presents
under all of them. (Laughter.)

Actually, that year there were twenty-seven White House Christmas trees!

of apples around the White House as a healthy treat, but would Santa appreciate apples? The President, the First Lady, and longtime supporter Oprah Winfrey discussed this very topic during a one-hour prime-time special on decorating the White House for Christmas, which the First Family granted the talk show queen.

⌒ MRS. OBAMA:
"Santa likes cookies. Maybe we'll put apple slices out, but . . ."

PRESIDENT OBAMA:
"Santa generally likes cookies."

MRS. OBAMA:
"Santa eats what he wants."
(Laughter) ⌒

That December there was a whirlwind of parties, and Mrs. Obama joked they had a hundred thousand guests over for the holidays. In the White House, though, there was also an emphasis on community service. The First Lady vigorously supported Toys for Tots, a program that Barbara Bush had also supported. Mrs. Obama urged Americans to remember preteen children, ages eleven to fourteen, whose bins remained empty at the Toys for Tots main facility in Quantico, Virginia, just days before Christmas. Mrs. Obama also touted the "United We Serve: Feed a Neighbor" initiative, which tried to combat hunger in America. As always, the First Lady advocated thanks, praise, and support of the military and their families.

For the Christmas holiday, the Obamas traveled with friends and family to the President's hometown of Honolulu, Hawaii, which they had been doing for many years. There a house full of noisy children played, visited the zoo, and swam in the ocean. One holiday tradition was a mandatory talent show. In past performances, the First Lady showcased her hula-hooping skills, and the President attempted to lip-synch popular songs, at which he confessed he was terrible.

Christmas 2010 brought Mrs. Obama's theme of "Simple Gifts," which highlighted the important things in life—family, friends, love, and volunteer service. "Simple Gifts" was also an appropriate theme given the harsh economic struggles many Americans continued to face that December. Again Mrs. Obama used the Christmas decorations to highlight the issues

LEFT :: The President and First Lady joyously greet Edith Childs from South Carolina, during a 2009 holiday reception. A campaign volunteer, Childs is credited with creating the slogan, "Fired up, ready to go!"

she felt were important. Elements of nutritious food, environmental consciousness, and the nation's commitment to its military troops were all reflected in the decorating.

In the Blue Room, the official tree was decorated with state fair ribbons from all over the United States, and bunches of wheat tied in light blue silk ribbon. Wheat, traditionally a symbol of life-affirming nourishment, also sprouted from the top of the tree like a crown. Students from the Savannah College of Art and Design made miniature pennant ornaments to accent the tree. In the Grand Foyer, two towering urns stood at the entrance to the Blue Room, one on each side. They were filled with soaring birch branches strung with white lights. Also in the Grand Foyer, two large evergreen trees were decorated in red and gold ornaments with rich red tree skirts.

That season the Green Room was truly green, with environmentally conscious decorations. Two tall standing trees were made entirely of recycled newspaper. Smaller table-top trees were made of recycled magazines and dusted with glitter. In the Red Room, the cranberry variations continued. Designers created a contemporary sphere that looked like cranberry topiary. The mantel was dressed with two complementary silk fabrics, on which natural elements like magnolia leaves were scattered, and round ornaments covered in cranberries were placed.

In the East Room, four large trees shared the room with the crèche. The trees were done in turquoise, purple, gold, and green. Fake peacocks and flowers settled on the branches. Perched atop each tree was a large peacock sculpted from natural elements like branches, dried hydrangeas, grass, and moss. In the State Dining Room, garlands of painted gold leaves and fruit dressed the room and two standing trees. Similar to the year before, the white chocolate gingerbread house re-created the White House, and it topped the scales at four hundred pounds. That year a larger-than-life Bo sat in front of the house. The pastry chefs explained that his giant proportions reflected the fact that his role at the White House had grown exponentially over the course of the year.

That year Mrs. Obama simultaneously threw the first party of the season for three hundred military families and held a press conference to describe the decorations to the media. The military guests were U.S. Marine Corps families who had volunteered tirelessly once again to make Toys for Tots a success. While the press toured the decorations, Mrs. Obama invited the children to the State Dining Room to visit a variety of craft stations. At one of the parties, children made homemade holiday cards, which they decorated by dipping stamps carved from vegetables into paint. At other stations, kids could make magazine Christmas trees like the ones in the Green Room, as well as other White House decorations.

One of the crafts was a project Mrs. Obama needed the children to make in order to complete the 2010 decorations. She asked each of the children to decorate an inedible

At one of the parties, children made homemade holiday cards, which they decorated by dipping stamps carved from vegetables into paint.

gingerbread ornament to complete a Children's Military Tree located on the ground floor. This tree complemented a nearby tree that was close to Mrs. Obama's heart, the Military Appreciation Tree, which had been decorated earlier in the week by another group of military children. Glass ornaments labeled "Army," "Navy," "Air Force," "Marine Corps," and "Coast Guard" hung on the red, white, and blue tree, along with balls in patriotic colors. A dove sat atop the tree, symbolizing the Obamas' desire for world peace. A basket of stationery was placed next to the tree for

visitors to write notes to American servicemen and servicewomen. The President and First Lady promised the letters would arrive overseas in time for Christmas

When the children went to hang their gingerbread ornaments on the Children's Military Tree, they also got to see the military tree that honored their parents. And while the children appreciated both trees, it was an altogether different sort of decoration that brought squeals of laughter. In an area Mrs. Obama designated the Children's Area, a large replica of Bo, made of forty thousand pipe cleaners, delighted everyone who saw it. Bo was so popular in 2010 with White House visitors that his paw print even accompanied the First Family's signatures on their official holiday card. The pastry chefs weren't kidding when they said Bo's role at the White House had grown over the year!

That year Christmas came early for Mrs. Obama. Since becoming First Lady, she had worked hard to focus attention on healthy nutrition for American children. On December 14, President Obama signed the Healthy, Hunger-Free Kids Act of 2010, which aims to provide nutritious lunches for American children, and eliminate hunger at school. The official signing of this act was a momentous occasion for the First Lady.

The same day the President signed the act, Mrs. Obama later visited the Children's National Medical Center. When the children asked what she wanted for Christmas, she replied:

⌒ One of the biggest gifts I got this year, I got it this morning. We signed an important law that helps make the school lunches more healthy, and that was my big Christmas wish. I was talking to Santa, "Oh please Santa, please bring this," and he did, so I got my gift early. ⌒

ABOVE :: Real-life First Dog Bo poses with a pipe-cleaner sculpture made in his likeness. The four-foot statue was made by eighty volunteers, who used forty thousand pipe cleaners.

RIGHT :: A plain plastic ornament was recycled to feature the President's home state of Hawaii.

The children then shifted their focus to the President. They wanted to know what she would give him for Christmas. The First Lady

Bo was so popular in 2010 with White House visitors that his paw print even accompanied the First Family's signatures on their official holiday card.

said she couldn't tell them, because she had made a pact with Malia and Sasha to never mention in front of the press what they were getting the President, because the press would tell him. Still, her young audience insisted on giving her gift suggestions. The First Lady smiled when one child suggested she buy the President an ornament, chuckled when another recommended a new suit, and burst out laughing upon hearing, "You should get Barack Obama a new hot tub." To which she replied, "You think he has an old hot tub?!"

On Christmas Day 2009 and 2010, the Obamas enjoyed their own new Christmas tradition, visiting military families as they gathered for Christmas dinner at Anderson Hall, on the Marine Corps base in Hawaii. Mrs. Obama felt honored each day by her role as the nation's First Lady, and she remained thankful for all her other blessings, which she worked to share with others, especially at Christmas. For Mrs. Obama, Christmas was not about material gifts, which she made clear in her holiday greetings:

⌒ On behalf of the Obama family, I wish all of you a joyous and meaningful holiday season! ⌒

THE OBAMAS' FAVORITE
Childhood Gifts

President and Mrs. Obama shared memories of their favorite childhood Christmas presents with Oprah Winfrey when they appeared on her talk show in 2009. Mrs. Obama got an Easy Bake oven she adored, but her favorite Christmas gift was a dollhouse. The future First Lady loved to spend her time arranging the furniture!

For his part, President Obama remembered a basketball that was given to him by his father on one of the few occasions he saw his father at Christmas. The President disclosed that his desire to do well in basketball was connected with a desire to please his distant dad. And reflecting more deeply, he noted that the love he grew to feel for the game mirrored the love he had as a young boy for his father.

Michelle Obama's
GINGERBREAD ORNAMENTS

I was delighted by the sweet smell of cinnamon as I made Mrs. Obama's gingerbread ornaments (pictured left). Mrs. Obama's gingerbread men are not edible, but they make a wonderful family project. After the gingerbread men have dried for a few days, children of all ages can help embellish them.

Supplies

Rolling pin or round glass bottle

Gingerbread man cookie cutter, 3 to 5 inches high

1 cup ground cinnamon

1 cup applesauce

¼ cup school or craft glue

Wax paper or plastic wrap

1 plastic drinking straw

Tip :: You can use buttons, ribbon, yarn, or fabric to decorate your gingerbread ornaments.

STEP *One* Combine the cinnamon, applesauce, and glue. Mix thoroughly. Dough should be stiff; add more cinnamon if it is too soft.

STEP *Two* Roll mixture between sheets of wax paper or plastic wrap to ¼-inch thickness.

STEP *Three* Cut out gingerbread shapes with cutter, and make a hanging hole with straw. Move to drying rack, paper towel, or newspaper. Allow to dry for 2 to 3 days, carefully flipping occasionally. Ornaments will lighten in color as they dry.

STEP *Four* When dry, decorate as you like!

REPRINTED WITH PERMISSION FROM
THE WHITE HOUSE

Selected Bibliography & Resources

Bauer, Stephen. *At Ease in the White House: Social Life as Seen by a Military Aide.* Lanham, Maryland: Taylor Trade Publishing, 2004.

Bush, Barbara. *Barbara Bush: A Memoir.* New York: Lisa Drew Books, 1994.

Bush, Laura. *Spoken from the Heart.* New York: Scribner, 2010.

Carter, Rosalynn. *First Lady from Plains.* Boston: Houghton Mifflin, 1984.

Clinton, Bill. *Bill Clinton: My Life.* New York: Alfred A. Knopf, 2004.

Clinton, Hillary Rodham. *An Invitation to the White House: At Home with Hillary Clinton.* New York: Simon & Schuster, 2000.

———. *Living History.* New York: Simon & Schuster, 2003.

Eisenhower, Julie-Nixon. *Pat Nixon: The Untold Story.* New York: Simon & Schuster, 1986.

Ford, Betty with Chris Chase. *Betty Ford: The Times of My Life.* New York: Harper & Row, 1978.

Johnson, Lady Bird. "Christmas Story." *Redbook Magazine*, final draft from White House Files.

———. *Lady Bird Johnson: A White House Diary.* New York: Dell Publishing, 1971.

Obama, Michelle and Barack, interview by Oprah Winfrey. *Christmas at the White House: An Oprah Primetime Special.* ABC, December 9, 2009.

Peterson, Charles. "The First Family & Christmas Memories." *Parade Magazine*, December 21, 1971.

Reagan, Nancy. "Our Last White House Christmas." *Ladies Home Journal*, December, 1988.

Rosenbaum, Alvin. *A White House Christmas.* Washington, DC: Preservation Press, 1992.

Smith, Marie. *Entertaining in the White House.* New York: Macfadden Bartell, 1971.

Temple, Dottie and Stan Finegold. *Flowers, White House Style.* New York: Simon & Schuster, 2002.

Warhol, Andy, Bob Colacello, and Doria Reagan. "A White House Christmas." *Interview Magazine*, October 14, 1981.

Weinraub, Judith. "Interview with the First Lady." *Washington Post*, December 8, 1982.

White House Christmas, HGTV, 1998, 1999, 2001, 2003.

Boston Globe
Los Angeles Times
New York Times
Washington Post

Brandywinemuseum.com
Clintonlibrary.gov
George W. Bush, Frozen in Time Official White House Website
The White House Historical Association: The White House Christmas Tree Themes
WhiteHouseChristmasCards.com
WhiteHouse.gov

THIS BOOK WOULD NOT HAVE BEEN POSSIBLE WITHOUT THE ENORMOUS HELP OF THE PRESIDENTIAL LIBRARIES. THANK YOU TO ALL THE DEDICATED PUBLIC SERVANTS WHO HELPED ME UNCOVER THE PRICELESS CONTENTS OF THIS BOOK.

John F. Kennedy Presidential Library: Maryrose Grossman, Keiko Makishma. **Lyndon B. Johnson Presidential Library:** Renee Bair, Barbara Cline, Tina Houston, Kristen Lambert, Christina Rodriguez. **Richard Nixon Presidential Library:** Pamla Eisenberg, Steve Greene, Melissa Heddon, Meghan Lee, Ryan Pettigrew. **Gerald R. Ford Presidential Library:** Samantha Ashby, Mark Fischer, Christian Goos, Tim Holtz, Nancy Mirshah. **Jimmy Carter Presidential Library:** Polly Nodine, Amanda Pellerin. **Ronald Reagan Presidential Library:** Kimberlee Lico, Michael Pinckney, Ray Wilson. **George H. Bush Presidential Library:** Mary Finch, McKenzie Morse. **William J. Clinton Presidential Library:** Rachael Carter, John Keller, Herbert Ragan. **George W. Bush Presidential Library:** Jodie Steck. **The 2011 White House:** Rick McKay, The White House Photo Office and First Lady's Press Staff. **The White House Historical Association:** Hillary Mannion. **The White House Office of the Curator:** Lydia Tederick.